ON EAGLE WINGS

by

Harriett Erickson

Blessings to you,
Harriett Erickson

ISBN 0-943167-07-8

Published by Faith & Fellowship Press

Dedicated with love to my wonderful family,

Jay, Jim and Joel

Special appreciation to Esther Fuglestad Stalsbroten for resource material from her experiences in the U.S. Army in SHAEF G-2 Headquarters (American Intelligence) under General Eisenhower during World War II.

And to my brother Marvin Syverson who served in the Tenth and Fourteenth American Air Force in Africa and China-Burma-India from 1942-1946.

Also to the Rev. Raynard Huglen for his great help in editing the manuscript for this book.

Harriett Erickson
2345 Jonquil Lane, North
Plymouth, MN 55441

Harriett Erickson was born in southern Minnesota. After graduation from college, she worked at the Mayo Clinic for five years.

In 1948, she married Pastor Jay Erickson. After traveling for the Hauge Innermission until 1956, they served congregations in South Dakota, Iowa, Washington and Minnesota, They have two sons. Jim is a pastor in Michigan and Joel is a corporate attorney in Minneapolis.

In addition to homemaking and parish duties, Mrs. Erickson has enjoyed teaching piano, writing books, and sewing. It is her prayer that this book might bring glory to God and be of encouragement to the readers.

Table of Contents

Chapter 1

Interruption

I awoke suddenly when torrential rain began beating on the roof of our log cabin, built at the edge of the Amazon jungle. The wind howled as it blew through the open window. Opening my eyes I saw light from the old kerosene lamp flicker ominously, creating eerie shadows on the primitive walls. I tossed restlessly on the crude bed and passed in and out of reality.

Only a few hours ago, a coffin carved out of a log by some natives was awkwardly lowered into the red Brazilian soil. Was it really my dear husband Steve in that coffin? Or could these recent happenings be merely a bad dream from which I would soon awaken?

Fear and gloom lurked outside the cabin. Inside, I struggled for breath in the hot, humid air while perspiration oozed from my forehead and trickled down my face. My hair felt wet and sticky.

How could life have fallen apart so completely? Only two weeks ago, Steve had been so alive and happy! Then without warning, malaria struck—and snuffed out his young life. Having been married only two years, I was now rudely pushed through the lonely gates of widowhood.

But the Lord had given me grace to have a short funeral service. As a group of weeping natives gathered around the coffin, I said we had come to Brazil to tell them about Jesus who is the Resurrection and the Life. And I would meet Steve again in eternity.

Then slowly our little procession had gone to the small plot where the coffin was lowered into the ground. There I shared a prayer in their native language. But everything seems so unreal!

Was it only this morning that I touched his stiff, lifeless body? But I still can't believe he is really dead!

"Dear God, I just can't understand this. You called us to come down here to put this dialect into writing so these dear people might know how to find eternal life in Jesus Christ. And now Steve is dead! Why? Why?"

My heart is crushed with pain. And to think that this aching heart had been such a happy heart on June 7, 1939. On that day, I had walked slowly down the long church aisle in a white satin bridal gown, clutching my father's arm.

Steve was standing near the altar of the church with his two brothers. He wore a new navy blue suit and smiled warmly at me. How I adored him. And this very special person with sincere brown eyes and curly auburn hair would soon be my own dear husband.

After the wedding prayer, Pastor Maier had said, "Ye two shall be one—until death do you part."

And now, terrible as it was, death had come and parted us. No, I simply cannot accept this painful truth.

Alone now in our little cabin, I again looked at the flickering light from the old lamp on the table. Unbearable silence hung over the empty room.

I had been alone, too, the morning of September 10, 1936. I was walking to my college class in German 101 at Midwestern College in Nebraska. While passing by a grove of white birch trees on campus, I accidentally dropped a couple of text books.

"Hey, let me pick those up for you!" exclaimed an energetic young man with sparkling brown eyes. He appeared out of nowhere, it seemed.

I smiled at this handsome stranger. He looked at me somewhat shyly as he handed me the books.

Sometime later he confessed, "The first time I saw you, I noticed your long, blonde hair, dreamy blue eyes and petite figure. And when you smiled, that cute little dimple appeared on your right cheek."

He then cleared his throat and impulsively asked, "How about meeting me right here—about four o'clock this afternoon? Maybe we could walk downtown for a couple of cokes at the drugstore, or something. What do you say?"

I hesitated for a moment. "But—but I don't even know your name," I stammered.

"I'm Steve Sanford from Center City, Nebraska. And you?"

"Ruth Monroe from Fairmont, New York."

"Delighted to meet you."

"Same here—and thanks for picking up my books."

"How about meeting me by these birch trees at four today—this afternoon?"

He was not one to waste time.

"Okay, I guess. It *is* a beautiful time of the year. I'll be back here at four."

"That'd be just great!" he answered with enthusiasm. Then I heard him whistling as he hurried on to his class in Greek at Trinity Seminary. It was about a mile away. Early this morning he had come to the large library at Midwestern College to do some special research work for a class assignment.

But later as he walked into his classroom, some doubts popped into his mind. *Would Ruth really keep her promise to meet him? Or would he be "stood up"?*

Meanwhile, I walked slowly toward the rust-colored stone building where my German class was held. I felt somewhat unsettled. Should I keep this date? What do I know about

Steve? Nothing . . . really. But he did have an honest-looking face.

"Suppose I can risk it—at least for this time," I muttered to myself as I entered the noisy classroom.

Usually, I listened carefully to the teacher, but today I had trouble concentrating on the conjugation of German verbs. And the hands on the big school clock barely moved. Would four o'clock ever come?

When it finally did, I headed for the birch grove. Steve was already there waiting and seemed glad to see me. At least I had kept my promise.

The cloudless, azure sky provided a pleasant setting for the trees, now dressed in autumn cloaks of red, gold, maroon and bronze.

As we strolled along together, Steve said, "Old Mother Nature is surely showing off today, isn't she?"

"You can say that again," I answered, then stooped down to pick up a shapely red maple leaf.

Time seemed suspended as we walked down University Avenue.

"What is so rare as a day in September?" he misquoted.

I looked at him and frowned.

"Oh, I guess the poet actually said, 'What is so rare as a day in June?' But how could any day in June compete with these fantastic colors?"

"Know what?" I answered. "These avenues of red and gold maples remind me of lines of soldiers ready to march in a parade. And their brightness almost hurts my eyes."

"That's for sure."

"It couldn't be a better day, could it?" I added, trying to keep the conversation going.

"Nope. Besides . . . fall is my favorite season. Not too hot--not too cold. And those wonderful football games!"

"I agree. And my whole family loves sports, too," I said.

"By the way, what are you majoring in?" he asked, trying to get better acquainted.

"Languages," I answered.

"How come?"

"Well . . . communication and reading are so important in life. And you?"

"Theology. I'm in my first year of seminary."

"So?" I probed.

"Since I was a kid of 12, I've wanted to be a missionary to some primitive tribe that hasn't yet heard about God."

"Quite a challenge! And plenty dangerous with cannibals and poisonous snakes--and all that stuff!" I added with a shiver.

Steve grinned. "Well . . . it's dangerous to drive a car, too, but we do it anyway."

"Good point," I agreed. His logic wasn't bad either. After the first day we met, we dated rather often. And before we realized it, colorful autumn faded into cold, bleak winter.

Then one crisp December evening, while on our way to a basketball game, I said to Steve, "Isn't winter beautiful . . . in its own way? Clear skies with blinking stars in the dark blue velvet heavens."

"Sure thing. And look at those evergreens! The mounds of snow resting on strong, bulky branches—so secure," he added.

"Reminds me of the peace and contentment of nature, trusting in its Creator," I replied.

Suddenly Steve grabbed my arm and exclaimed, "Hey, just got an idea! Let's go ice skating when the game's over."

"Where?"

"On Clearwater River. We can skate down that crooked old river for at least a mile," he replied.

"A neat idea! Perhaps it'll help clear out some of the cobwebs from my head."

"Honestly," he added, "we'd probably all do better with some good physical exercise before exams, instead of all that last minute cramming."

Although the game was exciting, I could hardly wait until it ended. Afterward, we hurried back to our dorms for our skates. Then for almost two hours, we cruised up and down the frozen river. By that time I was exhausted and found an old fallen log to sit on.

Steve soon came over and sat beside me, asking, "Any chance you could spend part of your Christmas vacation with us? My family has been asking when they could meet you."

It would have been impossible to look into his deep brown eyes and refuse. So I said, "I really must be with my parents for Christmas. But perhaps there would be a few days around New Year's."

"Hey, that's great! Then I'll drive us back here in Old Betsy."

I looked puzzled, so he added, "Old Betsy is my Model A Ford. Not much for looks, but real dependable."

* * * * * *

The long train ride back to Fairmont for the holidays seemed endless, but was well worth it. Being together with my parents, my older brother Tom and my younger sister Sue on Christmas Eve felt like a touch of heaven. How I missed them all during the school months in Nebraska.

And now I was reluctant to admit how much I missed Steve. Several times a day I wondered what he was doing--and thinking. Finally, early in the morning of December 30, I boarded a train bound for Center City, Nebraska.

The trip was long and boring with few people on board. My car was cold, so I kept my winter coat buttoned up. We traveled all day, all night, and then about 4 p.m. on New Year's Eve, the train pulled into the depot.

At first, I couldn't see Steve any place and began to worry. Heavy snow was now coming down. Was this going to be a real blizzard?

I got my luggage together, left the train and walked toward the depot. Then I heard Steve call out, "Over here, Ruth. Betsy and I are over here!"

Was I ever glad to see him! And he gave me a warm hug.

"We'd better hurry on home," he added. "It's beginning to storm and we need to get there while the roads are still passable."

With the visibility at nearly zero at times, we just crawled along. The three miles seemed like thirty, but we made it okay.

I liked Steve's parents at once. They made me feel so welcome. Steve sure resembled his father. Next I met his three brothers—Luke, age 20; Ken, 18; and little Mark, 8.

At dinner that evening, Mark quipped, "Can't understand what's wrong with Steve lately. All he ever writes about is you and where you two have been together."

We all laughed. I blushed a little, but really enjoyed the happy spirit in their home.

The following days we did some skating and tobogganing. It felt so invigorating being outdoors after many months of inside studying.

In the evenings we played some games or gathered around the piano and sang together.

These were special days, so I found it hard to think about going back to college. But Old Betsy managed to get us safely there on January 5.

January continued to bring one blizzard after another. How cozy to be inside, as the snow swirled around the large buildings and left high drifts outside.

In the lobby of the girls' dorm there was a fireplace. Steve often came over to visit me, especially on weekends. We loved to watch the logs spit and crackle in the fireplace. A nice place to talk and dream about the future.

The winter months passed by more slowly than the autumn ones. But with April came warmer temperatures and the inviting fragrance of fresh lilacs cheered us winter-weary people.

Both Steve and I had final exams during the last week of May. What a relief when they were over! Then on Friday evening we walked downtown for a soda together.

"Sure gonna miss you this summer," he said. "Looks like I'll be helping Dad on the farm again."

"Same here," I added, already feeling a pang of loneliness in my heart. "I'm needed at Dad's drugstore, primarily at the ice cream counter."

"Will you write . . . often?" he asked.

"Once a week—maybe more," I replied. Secretly, I wondered how I'd ever survive the long summer without seeing him.

"And I'll answer every one," he sighed. "But it's gonna be a lonely old summer."

The next day I got on the train bound for Fairmont. What an endless journey! Although I loved being with my family, this summer would be different. No Steve to talk with.

We spent many hot July evenings out on the open porch, hoping for a cool breeze to come along. Mother often made us some ice cold lemonade.

The summer passed by . . . slowly. And on September 8, 1937, Steve was at the depot when my train chugged in.

As I stepped off, he took my hand and exclaimed, "What a long, long summer that was!" Then he opened the door of Old Betsy and I climbed in.

"Thought it would never end, too," I said, gazing into his sincere brown eyes. "Funny thing . . . but in past years, the summers always seemed to just fly by."

He smiled and then suggested, "Say, let's stop at the Oasis for a sandwich and cup of coffee."

"Good! I'm starved after that long, boring train ride."

While we ate our hamburgers, Steve looked at me intently and said, "Let's talk about our future—together."

I looked at him, a little surprised.

"You know," he hesitated, "for several years I've had this strong feeling about going to Brazil—after finishing seminary. Do you think you could handle the primitive conditions down there?"

I took a deep breath, shivering at the thought of snakes, or even worse, cannibals!

"Can't say for sure now, but I'd be willing to try. The Lord gives grace for each challenge in life, I've learned."

"Well . . . I believe He wants me to go to one of the unreached tribes along the Amazon River and translate the Scriptures into their own native tongue. How else will they ever hear about salvation in Jesus Christ?"

"You're right. I remember one missionary saying, 'No one should hear the Gospel twice until all have heard it once.'"

"My feeling exactly." He smiled at me and squeezed my hand tightly.

After that day we saw a great deal of each other. What an enjoyable school year! Picnics, ball games, studying and praying together.

Then on May 20, 1938, I graduated from Midwestern College and decided to stay on for another year to get my Master's Degree.

There was a better reason, of course. I wanted to be near Steve . . . and he still had one more year of seminary left.

My graduation gift from Steve was very special. A beautiful diamond engagement ring. So that last summer in Fairmont, whenever I felt lonesome, I'd glance at my sparkling ring. It gave me assurance that the next June we would be together — forever!

The final school year went by rather quickly. Although we both studied hard, we took time to be together as often as possible.

Steve graduated from Trinity Seminary on May 26, 1939, and on June 7 we were married in my home church in Fairmont. The most wonderful day of my life!

But our honeymoon was destined to be something else.

Chapter 2

An Unforgettable Honeymoon

At this present painful moment, however, I was alone in the cabin. The hot, humid Brazilian weather made me perspire continually. As I drifted in and out of reality, my wet hair reminded me of another experience. My hair got even wetter then!

It all began after our wedding reception. Steve and I hurriedly changed into some casual clothes for our trip.

"Please tell me now where we are going on our honeymoon!" I pleaded. The suspense of not knowing was getting to me.

"Not yet! It's a surprise."

"Can't you even give me a hint?" I teased.

"Well . . . it's a real wilderness area—great for camping."

"Hmm . . . sounds interesting enough. But I hope we won't run into any snakes."

"I'll protect you, if we do," he answered gallantly while his brown eyes twinkled.

After putting our luggage into the back seat of Old Betsy, we climbed in front.

The day was perfect, but it was already five o'clock in the afternoon before we got going. We drove until ten o'clock and then found a cozy motel in a secluded area.

In the quietness of our small room, we talked about the joy of having our families and friends with us on our wedding day. It had been a busy day, so before long the whispering pines lulled us into a deep sleep.

We got up rather late and had a brunch at about ten. On we drove for two more days and enjoyed going through new towns we had never seen before. Each one had its own personality. Everything went well until we reached western Wisconsin.

Suddenly, there was a weird, scraping noise.

"Oh, oh," groaned Steve. "Sounds like a flat tire."

I sighed as Steve pulled over on the shoulder of the road. Sure enough, the right rear tire was very flat.

He took the jack out of the trunk, but had a real struggle loosening the rusty nuts from the wheel.

When the wheel finally came off, he discovered that the spare tire was also flat. He'd forgotten to air it up before we left. And here we were--miles from any town. What a way to begin a honeymoon!

"What do we do now?" I asked, looking at the two useless tires.

Steve looked around and soon noticed two horses prancing about in a nearby pasture.

"Has to be a farm near here some place!" he exclaimed with joy. "Maybe if I follow the fence line, I might find a house—or somebody."

While I sat in Old Betsy, Steve walked along the fence for a quarter of a mile. There in the distance was a two-story white frame house. He ran toward it. The farm also had a barn, silo and several other small buildings.

But when Steve entered the private driveway, he was suddenly met by a tall, bearded man with a rifle in his hands, who proceeded to fire a warning shot into the sky.

Steve froze momentarily. Then he blurted out, "Hey, friend, put down that gun! You see, my wife and I are on a trip to Minnesota and we just got a flat tire. The spare is also flat—so we really could use some help."

The gruff-looking farmer, dressed in a red plaid shirt and gray overalls, looked suspiciously at Steve for a while. Finally, he slowly put down the gun.

"Just wanted to make sure you weren't some gangster coming along to rob us," he explained. "Times are tough and ya never knows these days when someone like John Dillinger might be comin' around to gun us all down!"

Steve looked confused, but said nothing.

Then the farmer pointed east and said, "My tool shed's over thar. Should have an old air pump around some place."

"Thanks, I'd be much obliged," answered Steve politely.

"Young fella--just make sure ya bring it back when you're done," he warned, looking crossly at Steve.

They walked into a cluttered tool shed. After searching for awhile, the farmer managed to find his tire pump.

He looked it over, then added, "Guess I'd better put some friction tape on this hole in the rubber tubing. Seems to me the last time I used it, air kept getting out through that hole."

After a hasty repair job, he handed the pump to Steve, who thanked him warmly and headed quickly back to me and Old Betsy.

While whistling Steve thought to himself, *Glad that old boy didn't shoot first, then ask questions!*

As he came into view, he held up the pump for me to see.

I climbed out and stretched my legs. Steve put his foot down on its base and kept pumping up and down as fast as he could.

Finally, after ten minutes of that, he groaned, "Whew . . . this is hard work. Need a break now."

"Let me pump for a while," I offered. "It'll soon be dark, and I hope we can find a nice spot to camp before then."

"You really don't need to," he stated.

"Won't hurt me a bit. Besides—we'll both have to learn how to rough it when we get to Brazil!"

After several turns each, we finally got enough air into the spare and hoped it would get us to the nearest town--and gas station.

With the car running again, we drove back to the farm to return the pump. The man in overalls was waiting for us . . . leaning against his mailbox.

Steve got out and handed the pump to the farmer. "Thanks so much for helping us out. Hope we can make it now to the closest town."

"Just keep going north on this road," the farmer added. "Another 15 miles and you'll be in Reedsboro. Small place, but they got a gas station there."

Steve waved as we drove on in Old Betsy.

The spare held up till we came to the Webb Station in Reedsboro. After the attendant filled the car with gas, Steve then asked if he would fix our flat.

The man nodded and checked over the tire. A large nail had caused the problem. First, he patched the innertube. And at 15 cents a gallon, the cost of the gas plus fixing the flat came to $2.30.

Steve looked around and then asked, "Is there such a thing as a park around here where we could camp for the night?"

"You betcha! One block west and one north. Ya can't miss it."

We found the park and after a hurried supper of canned stew, crackers and grapes, we crawled into bed. I was exhausted.

The next morning, as soon as the sun broke through, we got up and went without breakfast. I took a nap while Steve drove on.

We stopped at a cafe in another small town for breakfast. Again I asked Steve, "Now can you tell me where we're going on our honeymoon?"

"To the Boundary Waters of northern Minnesota."

I wondered what kind of a place that was, but said nothing to him. Secretly, I would rather have roughed it in a nice motel instead of camping out.

The remainder of the trip through Wisconsin went quite well, except for having to add some water to the radiator once. Old Betsy must have had a small leak.

The scenery up the Gun Flint Trail was remarkable. And I made up my mind to learn to enjoy tenting.

Finally, as the last rays of the evening sun slid beneath the horizon, our Model A Ford pulled into a remote camping area. After registering with the caretaker, we soon found campsite No. 10.

Steve pounded down the stakes and raised the tent. By now it was dark and we were tired from the hot, dusty journey. How I longed for a nice cool shower. None here. I'd take a swim in one of the lakes tomorrow. At any rate, the cool pine-scented air soon put us to sleep.

The next morning Steve drove back to the caretaker's cabin about a mile from our tent. He rented a canoe for the day so we could do some fishing.

We portaged the canoe over to the nearest lake. The water was still . . . like a mirror. As Steve paddled away from shore, he asked, "How'd you like some fresh fish for supper tonight?"

"Great!" I answered.

At first the canoe felt rather tippy, but we soon learned how to balance it fairly well.

The azure sky and clear, clean water with lots of evergreens in the background made it a painter's paradise.

We fished all morning and into the afternoon, but caught nothing.

Steve looked at me and grinned, "These fish must be well educated. They seem to be able to eat the worms off the hooks without getting caught."

"They've probably had some good practice," I added.

As the sun was lowering in the west, we opened the sack lunch we had taken along. The sandwiches tasted good as we were hungry.

But suddenly Steve shouted, "Honey, I think I've got something on the line!"

"A northern?"

"Maybe . . . or a walleye."

After tussling with his line a while, he managed to land a four-pound northern pike.

"Can hardly wait to sink my teeth into this old boy!" he cried with delight.

We continued to fish for another hour, but caught nothing more.

Back at camp, Steve got a good fire going and fried the pike in an old castiron pan he had brought along. The enticing aroma of fresh fish frying in the open air made us both ravenous.

On our way up here while going through Duluth, we had bought some groceries, so I made a quick tossed salad. And the food really tasted great as we ate outside our tent. I now had to admit—camping was more fun than I had dared hope for. And sleeping in an airy tent was better than a hot, stuffy motel room.

The next three days we went hiking or fishing. Even found time for some light reading . . . plus getting better acquainted as we talked about our growing-up years.

The night before we were to drive back to Fairmont, I said to my husband, "If only this honeymoon would last forever."

He smiled and added, "It has been wonderful, but tomorrow we'd better head back to your folks and do some barrel packing for the boat trip to Brazil."

A month before we were married, the Outreach Mission Director sent Steve an official letter of call to work in Brazil. In the letter he also gave him an itinerary of five churches in New York and Pennsylvania which were interested in supporting a missionary couple. We planned to drive to these churches in Old Betsy.

About eleven o'clock that night we crawled into our sleeping bags. The Boundary Waters area was so quiet and peaceful.

Then about midnight, it happened. A heavy rainstorm suddenly struck.

As the fragile tent began to sway in the fierce wind, I asked Steve, "Do you think our tent will blow away?"

"Hope not. Maybe the storm won't last long and we can get some shut-eye."

After ten minutes of a soaking rain and driving wind, the gale seemed to let up. But then it returned with even greater fury. Jagged spears of lightning criss-crossed the sky, followed by loud crashes of thunder.

Then I shouted to Steve, "Believe I feel some water coming into the tent!"

"You're right! Where's the flashlight?"

"On top of the orange crate."

We had taken an old wooden orange crate along to put food in. It now served as a makeshift night stand. He also grabbed his billfold and my purse.

"The flashlight works," he added. "Now let's get out of here fast and head for Old Betsy."

But Steve just gasped when he turned the light on the car.

"Can't believe it," he cried, "but there's water already up to the windshield!"

"That's . . . that's impossible!" I exclaimed.

"But it's true! Here--grab my hand. We'd better head for the top of the hill. Must be a flash flood. And we'd better hurry up to higher ground before we get swept along with the strong current and drown."

"Is this a nightmare or is it really happening to us?" I asked.

"It's for real all right. Hey, follow me—and hurry!"

The night was pitch black, except for the small ray of light from the flashlight. But it kept us from falling over dead trees and other debris on the hillside.

We stumbled along for what seemed like an eternity before reaching the top of the hill.

"I'm freezing!" I added while shivering from the cold air and rain.

"No wonder. We're both soaking wet. Say, here's an old log. Let's sit down and catch our breath."

"How long till dawn?" I asked while my teeth chattered. "Probably several hours," he answered. "Here, let me put my arm around you. That might help some. With this terrible storm and darkness, we've no choice but to wait it out here till daylight."

"What if the water comes up this high?" I asked.

"Let's pray that it doesn't!"

Steve was mighty concerned, too. It seemed like a week before daylight broke. And I was painfully cold. But the storm was finally over. A clear, blue sky now greeted the dawn of a new day.

We walked barefoot down the hillside to where our campsite had been. Betsy was nowhere to be seen, for she was completely covered over with water. The tent and everything in it must have been swept down stream by the raging flood.

"I feel all sick inside," moaned Steve. "Like someone kicked me in the stomach."

"How little we know about what can happen in a few hours," I sighed.

My clothes and hair were dripping wet, as were Steve's.

"But Honey," he said tenderly, "we are very fortunate just to be alive." Then he gave me a warm hug.

Still barefoot and dripping wet, we stumbled on our way to the caretaker's cabin.

Because it was built on a high knoll, it survived the night's flash flood.

When the caretaker saw us coming, he ran out to meet us.

"Man alive, am I ever glad to see you guys! That was one terrible storm we had last night!"

"We know," agreed Steve.

He then continued, "The Peterson family was not as lucky as you, though. All six of them drowned when a wall of water struck their home and crushed it. They had lived only a mile north of us.

"How tragic!" exclaimed Steve. "I'm finding it hard to believe that this actually happened just last night. And the sunset had been so clear and beautiful."

"Did you save anything? What about your car?" asked the caretaker.

"We're okay, but the car is under water and our tent and other belongings were swept away with the raging current," said Steve.

"Even our wedding certificate went with the flood!" I cried.

He shook his head. Then added, "But at least you two survived. The whole Peterson family is now in the morgue. What a tragedy!"

Steve and I were simply speechless and still unable to grasp what all had happened only a few short hours before.

At that moment the caretaker's wife, Janet, came out.

"Come into the house right away," she said. "You two need to get into some dry clothes!"

"Bet we are a sad sight," I added, looking down at my wet and muddy pajamas.

"First off, both of you need a warm bath. Then we'll try to find something around here that might fit. We're heavier than you people, but we can 'make do' somehow."

She found us some clean underwear, then gave me a blue dress. Steve got a tan shirt and pants.

We were most grateful for these outfits and didn't mind the larger sizes.

They insisted that we stay here in their cabin while the water receded.

On the third day after the flood, the two men went to see Old Betsy. She was now standing in only a foot of muddy water.

"She sure looks tough," sighed Steve, finding it hard to believe all this had really happened.

The caretaker, who was also a mechanic, added, "With all that muddy silt now in the engine, it would cost ya more to fix her up than she's worth. Tell ya what. I'll give ya $25 and sell it for salvage."

"Fair enough," answered Steve. But tears came to his eyes when he looked at Old Betsy for the last time. She had been more than a car—she was a real, dependable friend.

That afternoon a truck from Duluth came to the cabin with the weekly supplies.

While unloading the food, the caretaker told the truck driver about our flood experience. He then offered, "Say, I'll be happy to give that young couple a ride back to Duluth, if they don't mind riding in my truck."

We thanked him and squeezed together in the front seat of the truck. It rumbled down the Gun Flint Trail, through Grand Marais, and finally to Duluth. The scenery was incredible — almost like the oceanside. We momentarily forgot about the costly flood.

When he dropped us off at the Greyhound Depot, he slipped a twenty-dollar bill into Steve's pocket. This, together with our own funds, was enough to buy two tickets to Fairmont. Fortunately, the night of the flood when Steve grabbed the flashlight from the orange crate, he also took along his billfold and my purse.

The bus ride back to Fairmont was tedious and hot. I often leaned against Steve's strong shoulder and tried to doze off. How I longed to see Mom and Dad and have a good cry!

The hours dragged by on the crowded bus. The temperature inside it felt like 95°.

What a relief when the driver at last called out, "Fairmont."

We walked the few blocks from the depot to my parents' home.

When Dad opened the door and saw us, he asked, "What in the world happened to you two? Where's your car?"

"A long story," moaned Steve. "We went camping in the Boundary Waters of northern Minnesota and got caught in a flash flood. Lost everything—but our lives!"

Taking a deep breath, Mother finally said, "Well, let's thank the Lord you both didn't drown!" Being very practical, she added, "Now we'd better get busy and sew you some clothes and other things you'll need in Brazil."

Hurting inside, I sat down by the kitchen table and cried, "What are we going to do now? And we have all those churches to visit, too!"

Chapter 3

Journey Down to Rio

The following morning after breakfast, Dad looked intently at Steve, then me. He said, "I'm going to take you dear people downtown today. Now, please . . . each of you pick out a nice outfit of clothes. They'll be gifts from Mother and me. You'll need something good to wear for your deputation work."

"But Dad, you needn't do that," I replied.

"I know, but it will be our pleasure to do this for two beginning missionaries."

Steve smiled while I gave Dad a big hug.

Later on as we walked into the spacious department store, I wondered what the clerks thought of the makeshift things we had on. No matter . . . I soon fell in love with an attractive rose suit and a pretty white blouse. Steve found a sharp-looking navy blue suit. After buying them, we also got some new shoes.

In the following days, what a lift those new outfits were, even though the trauma of the flood still gave us nightmares.

Steve went alone by bus to the three churches in Pennsylvania. At home Mom and I sewed some light cotton dresses, pajamas and so on. The Mission Board had sent us funds for supplies, so we also bought a tent, sleeping bags, tools, bedding, some canned goods and other things. These we packed into six large wooden barrels.

While packing, I thought about how much I would miss my family and friends. I loved all of them a great deal . . . including the entire community of Fairmont.

Mother frequently came down to the basement to see what progress I was making with packing.

She often said, "Sure am going to miss you when you go to Brazil." Then tears came to her eyes and she would choke up.

"And I'll miss you all, too, Mom! It hurts inside to think of leaving you and Dad, plus Sue and Tom, but we feel called by the Lord to try to bring the good news of salvation to those unreached people."

"How about language school?" she asked.

"The Board felt that as both of us studied Portuguese in college for three years, we could make it without further tutoring. Besides, the primitive natives down there don't even speak Portuguese, but some unwritten dialect. And we'll have to learn that from scratch."

I really missed Steve while he was gone, but did join him for the services in the two churches in upper New York. We traveled by bus, but sure missed the convenience of having our own car.

Then days of waiting . . . and waiting. If none of the churches took on our support, we'd probably have to look for some temporary jobs. Or accept a call to a congregation in the States.

Finally after ten long days, the Mission Director called, saying that the two New York churches had offered to give us total support (half each) so we could go to Brazil right away.

Steve grinned as he put down the receiver. "Honey, we're all set. The Board is sending us the boat tickets in a few days."

Therefore on July 27, 1939, Steve and Dad loaded up the six heavy barrels into the pickup truck and drove to New York harbor. Each wooden barrel had several metal straps on it. The trip ahead would prove to be tough on them—and us!

When they reached the harbor, the steamship *Juanita* was anchored there. The longshoremen were already loading cargo onto the vessel.

Dad and Steve returned home that same evening. Four days later Steve's family from Nebraska came and we all drove to the harbor. That very afternoon we began our exciting trip to Rio de Janeiro!

The big ocean liner gave a loud whistle as we tearfully said "goodbye." With some reluctance we then broke away and resolutely ascended the gangplank.

As she wiped her wet eyes with a small white hankie, Mom said to Dad, "It seems like they are going to the end of the world. We may never see them again."

"Now, now, my dear," he answered, "their future is in the hands of a loving God. We can trust Him for all things."

"I know that," she sighed, "but it still doesn't ease the pain of parting!"

As the *Juanita* glided out into the broad blue Atlantic, Steve and I stayed on deck near the railing, waving and smiling through our tears. Gradually, the mass of faces on shore faded from view.

Taking a deep breath, Steve asked me, "Wonder what's for dinner on this big old tub? I'm so tired from deputation work, I hope I can enjoy eating and get some extra rest during our long ride to Rio."

"Me, too," I answered. "I can hardly believe we are actually on our way to the Amazon country—with all of its challenges."

That first day at sea was peaceful and refreshing. The shimmering blue ocean waves slapped gently against the sides of the huge vessel.

However, quite unexpectedly about mid-afternoon on the second day out, a violent storm of near hurricane force suddenly struck the ship.

We watched the clouds above us churn ominously, changing from white into a sickening green and black. The lashing wind built up 40-foot waves at times, tossing the mighty vessel about like a cork on a torrent.

"Sure hope this old crate holds together so we can at least see the shores of Brazil!" exclaimed Steve, with a concerned frown on his face.

On the fourth day of the storm, I moaned to my husband, "This rocking motion is awful! I can't keep a thing down and the food they were serving was so good."

"Wonder if the crew will have to throw some of the cargo overboard to lighten the load?" asked Steve who looked rather alarmed.

"Worse than that . . . what if this ship breaks apart and we all go down?" I added. "It happens, you know."

Steve shook his head but did not answer me.

Although the captain of the ship tried to appear calm to the passengers, he inwardly feared for the lives of the people—and himself.

As the storm continued day after day, it was often accompanied by sharp flashes of lightning and loud, booming thunder. The huge waves beat against the hapless vessel continually.

Finally on the seventh day, after most of us had about given up hope, the wind calmed down. The tranquil evening sky turned into a deep coral, then paled into pink and silver shades. When darkness settled in, brilliant stars and a full moon adorned the blue velvet sky.

Steve and I were completely exhausted. We slept through the entire evening and on into the following day.

By late afternoon we awoke and were hungry. After putting on some dress clothes, we walked into the spacious dining room. The noisy, but relieved passengers crowded around the tables. For the first time I noticed the rich royal blue carpeting and lime green drapes there. Some of the people were almost giddy with relief that the storm was finally over.

Steve found a cozy corner table near a porthole and looked into my eyes. The romantic sunset of rose and gold colors soon melted into a deep purple while the sun quietly slid beneath the mighty Atlantic Ocean.

"Have I told you lately that I love you?" he asked tenderly.

"Yes, but keep on saying it every day, " I added, squeezing his hand.

We ate leisurely and enjoyed the gourmet food.

Later when we returned to our stateroom, Steve said, "Sure glad that hurricane is over, and I hope the weather behaves itself during the rest of the trip."

In the days that followed we discovered that most of the people were easy to get acquainted with. We soon made several new friends.

Then early Wednesday morning of our third week at sea, Steve gently shook me in bed. "Hey, look at those bright lights in the distance. Must be Rio. I can hardly wait!"

"Do you think they'll understand our Portuguese?" I asked rather apprehensively.

"We'll get by--somehow," replied my confident husband. "Let's get a hotel room first, then take care of some business. Maybe even do a little sight-seeing."

"There are so many places I'd like to see in Rio!" I exclaimed.

"First off, though, we'd better locate our ambassador. We'll need his help in getting our papers in order. And he might also know of some trustworthy guides we could hire to take us into the interior."

"Will it take long to clear customs?" I asked.

"Shouldn't. After all, we don't look like smugglers, do we?" he teased.

Shrugging my shoulders, I replied, "It's always the innocent-looking ones you need to watch out for!"

Steve laughed aloud and gave me a big hug.

"I can't wait to try my hand at bartering at those open-air markets," I added.

"Better be careful," he warned. "Some of those traders are plenty crafty!"

Suddenly my thoughts turned to the Amazon jungle and I asked, "Do you think there will be anything left of that deserted mission compound in the interior where we'll be going? Remember . . . the Mission Board told us some missionaries had worked there for only a short time many years ago."

"I have no idea what, if anything, is left, but we'll soon find out. Better be prepared, well . . . for almost anything!" he warned.

Chapter 4

A New Lifestyle

From the clock in our stateroom I noticed it was only 5 a.m. But we were already so excited that we jumped out of bed and hurriedly dressed for the great day ahead.

The engines of the *Juanita* slowed down to a crawl, as she glided smoothly into the Port of Rio.

Because it would take a few days for the ship's cargo to be unloaded, we planned to use this time for business and sight-seeing.

After clearing customs Steve registered us in the Sombrero Hotel, not far from the harbor. A taxi then took us to the American Embassy. In this stately white building we met the distinguished ambassador, Mr. Henry Stanley.

He helped us with the necessary paper work and also told us of two fairly reliable guides for our trip into the interior.

"But you simply must have a tour of our magnificent city before you do anything else!" he exclaimed. "One of my aides will be your host. He knows all the tales of intrigue and romance connected with wonderful Rio."

His hospitality was overwhelming—and appreciated. The week went by like a dream. So many interesting people, places and things to occupy our time. And we managed fairly well with the Portuguese language. But it would take time to become really fluent!

Steve finally located the guides, Juan and Carlos Cortez. They owned some mules and promised to take us and our supplies into the Amazon interior.

At the dock we got our six barrels, then bought more supplies, including food, and soon the mule train was ready to move out.

I was glad I had worn slacks when I tried to mount my mule. Steve scratched the long ears of his mule as she nuzzled her nose against his sleeve. Might as well make friends right away, he seemed to be thinking.

We paused for a final check of the barrels and baggage. I was anxious to get going, but not too excited about the rugged trail ride ahead. The thought of beginning our language work with the primitive natives would be sufficient motivation to help us over the rough times, so I thought.

The mules were heavily loaded down and plodded along slowly over the bumpy, winding road.

As we rounded a curve on the red, dusty road, Steve whispered to me, "No wonder these mules look so sad. It's tough going out here in the boonies!"

What a rugged trail. Hot, windy and bumpy. I wondered if I'd make it through the day. But even a Jeep couldn't have gotten far on this impossible terrain.

It seemed like an eternity before evening descended on the mule train. Then Juan called out in his broken English, "Stop here tonight. Good place to camp. Lake has good water."

"I'm so thirsty!" I cried. "My mouth feels gritty from all the wind and dust."

Carlos looked at me with a frown and said, "Make fire and boil water first. Not safe to drink from lake but animals can."

While Carlos hunted for some dry wood for a campfire, Steve staked down our small tent.

Juan had gone fishing and caught several, so we had fish, beans, bread and strong Brazilian coffee for supper.

Later on, after darkness had settled over our camp, I crawled into the tent with Steve. My back and legs ached from the bumpy ride.

"What I wouldn't give for a fly swatter," I moaned. "These flies and mosquitoes are just awful!"

"Pull the blanket over your head, Dearie. But let's hope some friendly snake doesn't crawl in with us tonight!" added Steve.

"Don't even mention the word 'snake'," I shuddered. "It's bad enough having all these insects chewing on me."

"They must like your sweet disposition," he teased.

I ignored him—this time—and hoped for sleep to overtake me. It didn't. The night was long and I was restless.

At daybreak Juan beat on a tin pan to awaken us. The countryside looked more impossible than what we had been through the day before. After breakfast we rode on, while the annoying red dust penetrated my nose, mouth, hair and clothes. But the heavy rain shower in the afternoon did not help our progress either.

That night when we made camp, I longed for the bathroom with a cool shower in Fairmont. But I had to settle for a dip in the river. That did help somewhat.

Every day brought new adjustments. The culture shock was really hitting me now. And I secretly wondered if I'd be able to cope with the heat, humidity, insects and other primitive conditions.

But after three weeks, the long trip over the rough terrain ended. We had reached our destination—and I had survived! Steve hurriedly looked around for any evidence of the old abandoned compound.

Twenty years had passed since the other missionaries had worked there. He picked up a large board that might have once been part of a table. Over to the right was one wall standing from a former building. But everything else was largely just rubble from rot and nature's relentless rains and driving winds. Whatever . . . it meant starting from scratch for us!

After unloading the stuff, Steve thanked the Cortez brothers and paid them. They smiled broadly and began tying the mules together with a long, thick rope. Now in single file, this entire mule train with their own supplies trudged back toward Rio.

As they were leaving, I ran over to the faithful mule which had carried me those many miles and petted his long gray nose. His sad brown eyes looked into mine, as he snorted out his own "goodbye."

After they all disappeared over the distant horizon, Steve said, "I'm getting an empty feeling inside. Now we are really alone in a strange, wild and possibly hostile land!"

I looked at him, but a big lump in my throat kept me from answering.

Just before they departed, Juan had warned Steve that in the nearby thick jungle growth lived a fierce Indian tribe, which had not been exposed to modern civilization, except during the three years when those other missionaries had lived on this very spot.

But that was two decades ago! At that time, two middle-aged couples from the States had arrived there and built a mission compound, consisting of a crude hospital, chapel and living quarters.

After working with the natives for only three years, one stormy night a group of warriors from a distant tribe staged a surprise attack. They killed all four missionaries, plus 13 men from the Indian village. They had come to rob, loot—and murder!

Since that gruesome tragedy, nobody else had volunteered to replace them. Until now. And we were young and inexperienced.

I felt overwhelmed by the awesome task of seeking to make friends with these savages. Then later on, we hoped we could learn their dialect and put it into writing.

After tenting that night, Steve said to me in the morning, "Looks like the first thing we must do is build a simple house for a base. With all the trees around here, a log cabin would be the easiest to make."

As he searched for the barrel containing some tools, I looked at him and said, "Sure glad you're here. I wouldn't know the first thing about building a house."

Steve grinned. "Nice to be needed, Kitten!"

We eventually found the barrel with the axe, hammer, saw and a few other tools. And soon the silence of the area was broken by the dull thud of one tree after the other crashing to the ground.

"Timber!" he shouted as each one fell.

Day after day I listened to the noisy chopping of balsa and pine trees, At the same time, the mosquitoes and other insects kept on bothering and biting us.

"What can we do?" I asked, while scratching a few welts on my arms and neck.

"Two things. Go to the drugstore for some insect repellent, or grin and bear it," he teased.

His sense of humor carried us over many tough situations.

The days stretched into weeks. But soon a crude cabin took shape at the edge of the Amazon jungle.

When it was almost completed, we moved our supplies, including the barrels, inside. The cabin would mean protection from the rain, wind, and noisy jungle animals. I had felt very insecure inside of our fragile tent when the wild animals had roared during the dark night hours.

The evening we moved into the cabin, I prepared a special meal for the celebration. A time of real thanksgiving.

However, just before we had our dessert, I squinted at the south wall. "Help!" I cried.

"What's wrong, Honey?" asked my bewildered husband.

"Look over there!" I added, pointing to the wall. "Those beady eyes!"

Steve quickly turned around and saw an inquisitive snake peering at us from between two logs.

He smiled and said, "Don't worry, Dear. If we don't bother him, perhaps he'll go away."

"I just hate snakes!" I exclaimed. "How can I sleep tonight thinking of that slithering old creature climbing into bed with us."

"Don't worry. As soon as I finish my dessert, I'll try to fill up that hole with some sticks and mud to keep him from getting in again."

I slept very little that night and dreamed about old beady eyes coming back into our house.

The next day I tried to push thoughts of snakes from my mind and busy myself by making our cabin somewhat cozy. I had brought along some print-colored flour sacks and sewed these by hand into some simple curtains over the open windows. A few calendar pictures which I had put in one barrel helped dress up the walls.

Steve now began working on a much needed "outhouse." When he was about half finished with it, he ran into a nest of bees in one of the felled trees. In their anger, they bit him several times.

When he came in for supper, he asked, "Do we have anything along to help with the pain and swelling from these bites?"

"I think I brought some baking soda along. Perhaps a paste made from that will ease the pain a bit," I replied.

Steve was grateful when the pain began to subside. Later on when the outhouse was finished, we made a rustic table, two chairs and a bed.

"I'll try to make more furniture in the future, he added. "In the meantime, we can use the barrels as makeshift cupboards."

The log cabin was very crude, but quite liveable. Much better than a tent!

But now we faced the reality of a visit to the unseen tribe living in the jungle. What did those people look like? Would they be fierce or friendly?

Several times Steve had said that he felt as though some of the natives were watching him from inside the jungle while he built the cabin. But no one ever came near us.

We needed to pray much before going to look for them!

Chapter 5

The Indian Village

With some real fear and trembling, one sunny day we cautiously trekked toward the native village. It was about a mile into the dense jungle growth, Juan Cortez had said.

As we walked into the heavy foliage, the branches slapped against our faces. Another new experience.

Finally we paused. Sitting in a circle on a partial clearing were a number of huts made from large branches. The natives outside were short, brown-skinned, with flashing black eyes.

The men had on loin cloths, while the women wore loosely woven grass skirts. Their jet black hair was shoulder length, with jagged-cut bangs across their foreheads. Some women also had small wooden discs hanging from their ears.

As soon as they caught sight of two strangers, five strong savages marched angrily toward us. Each one had a long sharp spear pointed directly at our chests.

They grunted, glared and then spoke rapidly in a foreign language. Steve and I smiled at them, hoping to convey a friendly spirit. The men also wore some red and blue paint on their faces. Were they getting ready for a raid or something?

The five warriors then stood tall and rigid.

Steve whispered to me, "Let's back out of here slowly and keep smiling."

I was so frightened, I nearly froze in my tracks.

Steve proceeded to pull me along as he moved backward.

"Not a good day . . . for visitation, " I said softly.

Suddenly on impulse, I took off my bracelet and offered it to the savage nearest me. I hoped he'd realize we came in peace. But the angry-looking Indian shook his head defiantly and grunted, "Ugh!"

Next, all five warriors shook their spears and began walking faster toward us.

So we moved quickly backward toward the thick jungle. Once in the heavy foliage, we ran a zigzag course toward our cabin. We didn't stop running until we got inside our house. Then Steve looked outside, but saw no one following us.

Steve pushed our home-made table against the door and said, "My knees are still shaking! How about you?"

I just nodded, too out of breath to talk.

He continued, "Perhaps they think we are so frightened, we'll never go back there again."

"And that's probably true," I moaned, trembling like a leaf.

What a disappointing first meeting with these primitive people!"

Steve was quiet for a while, then said, "Let's devote tomorrow to fasting and prayer. Only the Lord will be able to help us in this situation."

To add to our uneasy feeling, we heard the ceaseless, mournful beat of jungle drums during the next two days and nights.

"Aren't they ever going to stop?" I moaned, as we lay on our bed in the eerie darkness. "It's getting on my nerves!"

"This is just a guess," Steve replied, "but maybe they are getting ready for a big raid on some distant tribe. Did you notice that war paint on their faces?"

"Hope they hurry up and go," I said. "This drum beating is becoming unbearable."

But the drums pounded away all that night. Finally at daybreak of the third day, they suddenly stopped.

Then we heard blood curdling screams, followed by a deathly silence.

The strangely quiet morning passed by slowly. At noon I said to Steve, "Just got an idea. Why not bring some costume jewelry with us and go back to the village? The women and children must be alone now. Maybe we could try to win their friendship in this way."

"Hmm . . . worth a try," replied Steve, as his eyes brightened.

For no special reason, I had put a box of rings, bracelets and necklaces that I had accumulated as past gifts and put them in a box in one of the barrels.

So that same afternoon I brought this container of jewelry along, as we once again prayerfully trekked back into the thick green jungle.

Near the village, we cautiously peered through the branches. Several small children were playing in the dirt. I slowly walked toward a pretty little girl of about eight years, smiled and handed her a bright, shiny bracelet.

At first, she just looked at me and stared, wondering if I were only teasing her. But I gently put it on her right arm. Her big dark eyes opened widely and she smiled at me.

After looking intently at it for a few minutes, she ran into one of the thatched huts and showed it to a woman, probably her mother. Soon both the mother and girl peered cautiously out the doorway. Steve and I smiled and walked toward them. He then handed the mother a pretty necklace with pink, green and blue stones in it.

The mother was a little reluctant, but finally put it around her neck. She smiled and soon ran into her neighbor's house to show them the gift she had just received.

Before long, a number of women came out of their huts to look us over. Fortunately, we had enough jewelry along to give each one a present.

Shortly thereafter, one young mother handed Steve a bunch of ripe bananas. Then she beckoned us to come into her little house. We all sat on floor mats, while the mother told us the names of her three children.

The afternoon went by quickly, as several of the village women warmed up to us and tried to communicate by sign language. They seemed pleased with the gifts from another culture.

When the shadows lengthened in the late afternoon, we gestured that we needed to return to our own home. When we waved "goodbye" to them, they smiled and waved back.

This time Steve whistled as we struggled through the thick jungle growth. He grinned and said, "Well, Honey, we seem to be making friends with the women and kids, at least."

And we were thankful to the Lord for this small beginning in the great challenge before us.

Inside our cabin, I said, "Sure hope the women can convince the men of the tribe that we are harmless . . . when they return from wherever they went."

The next two weeks we stayed put. Letters and reports had to be written, plus making a few other pieces of furniture. I also went down to the river bank and washed clothes.

But soon it was time for another visit to the village. As we came near the jungle, disturbing thoughts plagued us. Would the warriors be home? Would they capture and torture us or tolerate our company?

Near the village we carefully peered through the thick foliage. The men had returned. But with the war paint now washed off, they didn't appear quite as fierce. I really hoped that the gifts we had given the women would convince the men that we came as friends.

The moment of truth arrived when we walked into the village. Suddenly, the little girl to whom I'd given the sparkling bracelet saw us and ran toward me. She smiled shyly and held up her arm to show us the bracelet.

Some of the men looked at us suspiciously, but at least they didn't pick up their spears this time!

We also noticed that several of the women were wearing the jewelry we had given them. The one with the colorful stones in her necklace invited us into her hut. There was a man inside, most likely her husband. He was carving some kind of animal from a piece of wood. He didn't even bother to look up.

We tried to communicate with the woman by hand gestures, but it wasn't easy. We smiled a lot, hoping they would realize we were here in the spirit of peace and friendship.

We kept our visit short. As we neared the door, the man put down his carving and spoke. We couldn't understand what he said, but the tone of his voice was rather pleasant.

The children playing outside accepted us quite easily and showed us some of their crude playthings.

About three in the afternoon, Steve whispered to me, "Perhaps we should go now . . . not wear out our welcome, you know."

So we slowly made our way through the thick jungle and toward our cabin.

That evening we had a prayer time of thanksgiving. It appeared that some of the villagers were friendly and others at least tolerated the two white-faced strangers.

After that day of seeming breakthrough, we went to the village about twice a week and soon learned the name of the mother of the little girl who received the sparkling bracelet. It was Coruma.

In addition to this girl of about eight years, she also had a son, whom we guessed was around 12. These two, plus some of the other children, were of real help in our learning words of their language. Coruma was busy with many daily jobs, but tried to take some time to help us.

We began by pointing to objects such as a tree, house or bowl. Then Coruma or one of the children spoke the name of it in their dialect.

As the weeks went by, words developed into phrases and short sentences. But the village men did not care to be involved at all.

We spent long hours in our cabin doing the needed homework. It was grueling and often discouraging, but we kept at it for almost two years. We estimated it would involve at least another three years before a primer would be ready. Then perhaps 10 more years to translate the New Testament into their native tongue.

* * * * * *

At the present moment in the cabin, however, I had to face up to the crushing reality of Steve's death. Over and over again, I cried out, "Why, Lord? Why should he die . . . just when we were making good progress here? It isn't fair at all!"

Sitting on the edge of the bed, I pushed back the wet strands of hair from my face.

"What can I do here now—all alone?" I sighed. Finally I forced myself to get out of bed and make a strong cup of coffee. Although it had taken me about six months to learn to drink the thick, strong Brazilian coffee, I had managed that.

Letters to us from the States had always been scarce and slow in arriving. When we first came to Rio, Steve had arranged with a bush pilot to fly out to our cabin once a month to bring us supplies and the mail. This was so important!

As I sat by the rough, homemade table, my warm tears dropped on the sheet of paper. I was trying to write the Mission Board about Steve's tragic death from malaria. But I couldn't seem to get the words into coherent sentences. And it would be yet another seven days before Pete, the pilot, would fly in for his monthly visit. There was no other communication here with the outside world.

What should I do now? Plenty! I felt reasonably sure the Board would order me to return to the States as soon as possible.

They would assume this was no place for a white woman to live alone.

With that thought in mind, I began sorting and packing a few valuables, along with some clothes in one suitcase. In the other one, I put the precious manuscripts—two years of hard work in this difficult tribal language.

As each lonely day faded into the next, my subconscious mind tried to convince me that I was only having a bad dream. Steve would be home any minute now, wouldn't he? Such an important task simply could not end this way!

When Monday finally came, I went outside several times in the morning, searching the clear blue sky for a sign of Pete's small aircraft.

Then I made my last visit to Steve's grave. As I knelt beside the mound of fresh dirt with the wooden cross on top, I cried softly. Everything was so unreal . . . like living in a perpetual nightmare.

"Oh, Lord, I need your help desperately . . . just to go on," I prayed. An hour passed by before I could leave his grave.

At last in the late afternoon, I heard the distant buzz of a plane. It was Pete's. Never before had his arrival been so welcome.

After he landed, Pete gingerly climbed out. I ran to meet him and with choking sobs told him what had happened.

He just gasped, staring at me in utter disbelief. A month ago Steve had chatted with Pete . . . and had been so alive and cheerful.

"Ruth," Pete insisted, "you simply cannot stay here by yourself one minute longer. Come back with me to Rio. Have you packed yet?"

"Yes, and I have a letter to mail to our Mission Director."

Pete wrinkled his nose, scratched his head and suggested, "Instead of sending that letter, why don't you just cable them from Rio. That way you'll get an answer in a couple of days."

"Good thinking, Pete. It's so hard to make decisions these days . . . and even harder just to make myself keep going. But I'll feel better when I hear from the Board directly."

Anxious to get going, Pete hurried into the cabin and picked up my two heavy suitcases. He groaned as he tossed the baggage into his plane, then helped me climb into the seat behind his.

At that moment, several of the natives who had heard the plane come in, hurried out of the jungle. They cautiously looked at the big metal bird.

I waved to them, then broke down and sobbed.

Coruma ran toward me and blurted out in her own language, "Come back soon! Help us learn to read and write. Tell us more about your God."

The other natives whispered to one another.

One young brave pointed to the plane and asked in his own dialect, "How can large bird carry people? Then fly into sky. Mighty strange!"

Pete looked puzzled, so I translated the message to him. These Brazilians were awed by the peculiar invention of a modern culture. But we didn't have time to explain anything to them now.

After Pete yanked the propeller down, the engine started. Then he climbed into the cockpit and we flew off from the narrow clearing.

The confused natives watched the silver plane gracefully lift off the ground and glide out into the bright blue sky.

Looking at the small group below, I wondered, *Who will take up our unfinished task? And will this ache in my heart ever go away?*

While we flew over the dense jungle below, I cried, "Lord, I need your comfort—to ease this terrible hurting in my heart."

Pete could not hear me as the steady drone of the plane's motor was almost deafening.

Later on, as the bright rays of the setting sun broke through the gold and purple clouds behind us, these words of encouragement came to mind, "But those who hope in the Lord shall renew their strength; they will soar on wings like eagles" (Isaiah 40:31).

Remembering the lonely cabin and fresh grave I left behind, I thought, *Will I ever return to these dear people so they can learn more about God's way of salvation? What lies ahead. . . for them . . . for me?*

Chapter 6

Healing and Upheaval

As the darkness thickened, I looked down from the small plane and could hardly see the serpentine river below in the moonlight. But the huge green jungle seemed to be choking itself in overgrowth.

My tired body and mind cried out for rest. Because of the pain of leaving Steve's body in that crude grave, my nerves had stretched to the breaking point. I closed my eyes and hoped for sleep to come. It did not. Finally about four hours later, the twinkling lights of the bustling city of Rio appeared in the darkness. Some flimsy blue clouds floated past the beautiful yellow moon.

In the distance we saw Sugar Loaf Mountain and the imposing statue of Christ with His outstretched arms. Oh, how I needed the comfort of those arms right now!

Pete guided the plane into a graceful landing. After turning off the engine, he swung himself down onto the concrete runway and helped me get down.

When he set my heavy suitcases on the runway, he sighed, "Do you by chance, have any rocks in these two?"

I tried to smile through my tears.

"Say, my car is over there. Why don't I take you to the depot so you can send that cablegram right away?" he asked.

"Good idea. And Pete . . . how can I ever thank you for all you've done for us?"

"'Twasn't much at all."

"After I send the cable, I'll get a room in the nearest hotel and try to get some rest before taking a ship to New York," I added.

"You should get an answer from that Mission by tomorrow afternoon," he said. "By the way, how are you fixed for cash?"

"I'm okay. Got enough for the hotel room and my trip home."

"Good girl! And say, I'll put my phone number on this piece of paper. Call us if you need help. Even if I'm gone, my wife will be home."

It did not take long to get to the depot in Pete's old car.

After he let me off, I entered the large ornate building. Sitting on an empty wooden bench, I scribbled down this message: STEVE DIED FROM MALARIA STOP NOW IN RIO WAITING ORDERS STOP RUTH SANFORD.

At the ticket window I handed the slip of paper to a short, black-haired agent. He wiggled his dark thick moustache, took the message, and said, "Why not check back here tomorrow about five in the afternoon? Might have an answer by then."

I paid him and left. More strange faces came into the depot. But loneliness gripped my heart even tighter.

Then in the distance I saw a phone and called the steamship company.

"Do you have a boat going to New York City soon?" I asked rather anxiously.

"Well . . . let me check," drawled a tired-sounding ticket agent. "This is Monday. Yes, we have one leaving on Thursday at 10 a.m."

"That's wonderful!" I exclaimed.

"Do you want a reservation on the *Queen Valeria?*"

"Yes, sir. And my name is Ruth Sanford."

As I walked out of the busy terminal, my body ached all over. So many people around me, yet I just wanted to find a room to be alone and cry my heart out. When Steve and I had been here two years ago, Rio had been so fascinating. But now, it was awful! A young widow . . . and all alone.

Taking a deep breath, I forced myself to carry the luggage across the street to the hotel. It didn't look so great but was handy.

After entering the lobby, I registered and a bellhop quickly picked up my suitcases. He took me to a small room on second floor.

After he left, I locked the door and sat on the bed. Then the emotional trauma of the past few weeks hit me hard. Too tired to eat, I simply lay down on the bed and slept . . . for the next 16 hours.

When I finally awoke, I blinked my eyes and squinted at the clock. Could it really be two o'clock on Tuesday afternoon? Impossible but true.

Now my growling stomach reminded me of how famished I was. But first a shower. What a delight to have running water again, even though it was cold.

Life near the Amazon had been so primitive. We got our water in pails from the river. Steve and I had battled mosquitoes, snakes and mildew, plus the other difficult conditions. Yet we always encouraged each other through days of despair and sickness. Dysentery came often and was hard to get rid of.

But the refreshing shower lifted my sagging spirits — somewhat. I put on my royal blue tunic dress and walked down the stairway to the coffee shop.

The aroma of brewing coffee met me as I sat down on a stool near the counter. The waiter took my order and soon returned with eggs, toast, juice and thick Brazilian coffee.

Although the food was delicious, I found it difficult to eat by myself. Would I ever be able to cope with life without Steve?

After the lunch I strolled out on the crowded sidewalk. I saw faces from many different cultures . . . German, Japanese,

Portuguese, French and Indian. Many eyes spoke of sadness and want.

To help push these thoughts aside, I visited a number of stores. One lady clerk had soft brown eyes, wore a white blouse, red vest, and long, flared black skirt. Very attractive.

One counter had some beautiful pottery for sale. Delicately painted plates and cups. There were all kinds of bowls and vases on another shelf. But I ended up buying a wood carving of a llama as a souvenir.

For the moment, my window shopping helped ease my sorrow. But when I headed toward the depot, the reality of leaving Steve's body near the Amazon River and the memory of those dear Indians pleading with me to return made my stomach churn. Should I really go back to New York and my parents or return by myself to the jungle? If only there were someone I could talk to . . . someone who really understood!

At the depot, I again went to the ticket window, told the agent my name and he handed me a yellow envelope. It was from the Mission Director. As expected, he ordered me to return to New York at once. That was my answer for now . . . to go home to my parents.

I hurried back to my hotel room and tried to read a book. But nothing made sense. I was still very tired from lack of sleep, so went to bed early.

In the morning I called Pete. He was gone, but his wife Rosalie answered.

"Please tell your husband that the Mission Board cabled me to return to the States," I said. "I'm booked to sail on the *Queen Valeria* tomorrow at ten o'clock."

"I'm so glad to hear that, my dear," she replied.

"I can never thank Pete enough for all his monthly trips with our supplies and mail," I added.

"He loves flying and enjoyed doing it, I'm sure. But . . . we both feel so badly about Steve's death—so untimely!"

My voice quivered and I couldn't say any more. I just sobbed. Rosalie understood, tried to comfort me and then graciously said, "Goodbye."

Later on during the evening while alone in my tiny hotel room, I set the alarm clock for 7 a.m. I couldn't afford to oversleep tomorrow.

That night I slept poorly and woke up several times and checked the time. When the alarm finally went off, I got up, showered, had a light breakfast and called a cab. The driver took me to the dock and even carried my two suitcases directly to my stateroom.

Soon the *Queen Valeria* glided out of the Port of Rio. I stood alone on the expansive deck. To boost my morale, I had put on my favorite rose-colored suit with the white ruffled blouse. (The one my parents bought for me after our flood experience). It felt so good to let the cool ocean breeze blow gently through my hair.

Gazing out into the endless Atlantic, I wondered what lay ahead. A long life . . . a short one? Loneliness or fulfillment?

As the ocean liner sped swiftly onward, I secretly wished that we would not encounter a storm like the one that battered the *Juanita* on our way down to Rio. I just wasn't able to handle one more crisis—right now!

On board, I spent some of my time trying to read. I bought a few magazines and had several books in one suitcase. But it was only My Bible—God's remarkable Word—that gave me the comfort I needed. The Psalms were especially meaningful. From them God seemed to say, "Trust Me, even when you don't understand My ways."

During the two long weeks at sea, I often walked on the deck and gazed at the beautiful turquoise sky, while the gushing white-capped waves slapped against the large vessel.

However, as soon as I returned alone to my room the pangs of loneliness and grief appeared again. Why should Steve have to die now . . . only in his twenties? Why is life so mysterious and so often full of tears?

The voyage seemed endless, but at least we had clear sailing.

Finally the day came when we steamed quietly into New York harbor. I was so anxious to see Dad and Mom as I really needed somebody to love and encourage me.

After the gangplank was lowered, I soon found myself being pushed forward by the press of passengers behind me.

The weight of the two heavy suitcases was getting unbearable, when suddenly I heard a voice cry out, "Ruth, Ruth . . . over here!"

When I saw Dad I dropped the luggage and just hugged him. Mother was along, too, but none of us could talk. We just cried together in both sorrow and joy. Happy to be together, but sad that Steve was not along . . . and never would be again.

Dad then cleared his throat and sighed, "Let's go home now. The traffic will be worse later on."

He gallantly picked up both suitcases and we walked toward the car.

Tears came to my eyes when I saw our old black Ford. So many pleasant memories with that car. But now there was so much to tell and I didn't know where to begin. If only Steve were with me! Before long I would also need a job to support myself. And jobs were scarce these days.

The ride home was rather quiet. But I did manage to talk briefly about the last days before Steve's death. How painful to relive them!

However, as we came into our familiar driveway, I felt a cloud of comfort enveloping me. Home again with loved ones. Surely it was the right place for healing and beginning life over again.

We entered through the kitchen door. And soon Mother began fixing one of my favorite meals—ham with pineapple rings, baked potatoes and sour cream, fresh garden peas, and chocolate pudding, topped with whipped cream and a red cherry.

I surprised myself and my parents by eating a hearty meal. The warm surroundings and stability of home were wonderful. But no one would ever be able to take Steve's place in my heart.

During the dinner hour Dad explained, "Tom is in Pittsburgh and will drive over here this weekend. Sue is having her final exams at Northeastern College but will also come on Friday.

"I can hardly wait to see them!" I exclaimed.

Then I began talking about the progress on our Indian language project, as well as some of the experiences during our last months together.

By eleven o'clock, I was too tired to continue, so climbed the stairway to my old bedroom. Nothing had changed. The walnut bed, dresser and cedar chest were the same. They reminded me of my very happy childhood.

When Friday came, we heard Tom's car squeal to a sudden halt. He ran through the door and hugged me so tightly I could scarcely breathe. Sue was right behind him and kissed me tenderly. Tom had met her at the bus depot and brought her along.

"How are you doing—really?" he asked softly.

"Quite well, thanks. Must admit, however, there have been times when I thought I couldn't go on, but the Lord in His Word reminded me of His strength for all our trials."

"Sure wish we could have been with you to help when Steve died, but, of course, we didn't even know about it until the Mission Director called the folks when he got your cable," added Tom.

"I'll never forget the shock of touching his cold and lifeless body. I ran to get some of the natives who then carved out a coffin from a big log. We had to bury him the same day because decay begins right away in that hot, humid climate."

"Were you able to bring along the manuscripts you had worked on?" asked Sue.

"Yes, I managed to collect all the papers and put them in one of the big suitcases."

"Are you going to take them to the Mission Headquarters for safekeeping?" Tom continued.

"Yes . . . the first chance I get to go to New York City. I do hope some couple will replace us soon. These manuscripts should be helpful to them."

It was now early in June of 1941. Already much of Europe was at war with Germany. And even the United States had begun drafting young men for military service. Would we soon be personally involved in this terrible war?

In one of his regular radio fireside chats, President Franklin Roosevelt had promised, "American mothers, your sons will never fight on foreign soil!"

How very wrong that statement soon proved to be.

The lazy days of summer sped by as I applied for several teaching positions in eastern New York, including Fairmont.

Quite unexpectedly on August 3, the superintendent at Fairmont's Lincoln High School called and offered me a job. It so happened that Mr. Kraus who had been teaching both German and French for the past five years was suddenly drafted for military service.

I accepted at once—a real answer to prayer.

On Tuesday morning after Labor Day, I met my students for the first time. I hoped they wouldn't notice how nervous I felt. This would be so different from working among primitive natives in the Amazon region. These bubbling and mischievous teenagers appeared to be quite a challenge—and they were—in the days to follow!

However, the many school activities filled my days to overflowing. And soon I noticed some of the frozen edges around my heart gradually melting away.

Nevertheless, the evenings were more difficult. I often cried myself to sleep and wrestled with the thoughts of why Steve should die so young when he was so needed in Brazil. Did God have something else for me to do and, if so, how could I find out what it was?

Because Lincoln High was only a short distance from our family home, I decided to stay with my parents for this school term, at least.

Autumn came—my favorite season of the year. Each afternoon I took a different route home. There was so much beauty in nature to absorb before the cold winds of winter settled in upon us.

I loved the birch trees flaunting their bright yellow leaves and white trunks. The stately maples wore cloaks of red and gold, while sturdy oak trees carried capes of maroon and bronze.

As I breathed deeply of the crisp, fresh air, I wished that Steve were walking beside me to share this beauty.

But soon Thanksgiving came and then I really looked forward to Christmas—with Tom, Sue and my folks—all of us together again!

However, there came an unexpected jolt. On Sunday afternoon, December 7, I had gone up to my room for a little rest. The past weeks had been hectic with tests and holiday preparations. My head ached.

I stayed in bed until five o'clock, then turned on my radio. An excited commentator blurted out this astounding news:

PEARL HARBOR WAS BOMBED BY THE JAPANESE AIR FORCE EARLY THIS MORNING. HEAVY CASUALTIES AND DESTRUCTION WERE EXPERIENCED BY THE AMERICANS THERE.

Quickly I sat up and turned up the volume. More and more details of the brutal attack were given.

Without even putting on my shoes, I raced down the stairway, touching only every other step.

"Dad! Mom! Did you hear the terrible news? Is it really true?"

Dad looked at me sadly and shook his head. "Guess it's true all right. But . . . somehow I really can't grasp the fact that this awful thing has happened to our country."

All three of us then hurried into the living room. Mother turned on the large console radio there. All regular programs were canceled as they gave more gory details of the slaughter and destruction of Navy ships and airplanes.

That evening President Roosevelt spoke to the nation by radio "Hundreds of American boys are lying dead in Pearl Harbor! Many ships and airplanes are also sunk or destroyed. December 7, 1941, is a day that will live on in infamy!"

How devastating! And just when life had become somewhat normal for me. Over night this tragic upheaval hurled our entire nation into chaos. How would it change the lives of people in the States? In the world? In our own family?

Chapter 7

An Opportunity

The winds of war blew fiercely across much of our planet. Its tempo had increased since 1939, the year the Nazis crushed Poland. Soon Belgium, Holland, Denmark, Norway and France also fell like dominoes as the German War Machine roared through them.

But the former impersonal war became very personal to us with the surprise attack on Pearl Harbor by the Japanese. It seemed that war madness had gripped almost the entire globe.

Even easy-going Lincoln High changed overnight. The carefree spirit became one of shock and seriousness. Several senior boys did not wait for graduation in May. They immediately enlisted in the Marines, Army or Navy.

Quite unexpectedly, I found myself teaching a very unpopular subject—German! The Monday morning after Pearl Harbor, I had just entered my classroom when a freckled-faced boy with a heavy shock of red hair yelled through the open door. "Hey, you Krauts! You oughta be spendin' your time studying somethin' better than this for your country!"

Looking at my bewildered students, I said, "Class, what happened yesterday is going to have drastic and heartbreaking consequences for all of us in the months to come. Life will never be the same again!"

The Axis powers of Germany, Italy and Japan seemed intent on conquering the world—at any cost!

Here in the States, rapid changes now began. Gasoline rationing. Thirty-five mile an hour speed limit for cars. Sugar and meat rationing. Auto assembly lines changed quickly into factories making bombers, fighter planes, tanks and warships.

Because these new industries offered high wages, many families sold their homes or farms and moved to the West and East Coasts. Some for the better-paying jobs, others to be near loved ones living on military bases.

Uproot . . . adjust . . . cry yourself to sleep. This was the new lifestyle of the early 1940s.

Only two senior boys from Lincoln High registered for college in the fall. The others had already enlisted in the Armed Forces or gotten temporary jobs while waiting for their draft number to be called up.

The only bright light from the Pearl Harbor tragedy was a new strong national unity. Our homeland had been savagely attacked by a foreign power. And we quickly united to fight for survival!

At this time most of us knew little or nothing about the Japanese or their culture. However, we learned a lot very quickly. The young American prisoners of war were often tortured or brutally slain. Unbelievable, yet true horror stories filtered back to the States from the war correspondents. One of the most popular ones was Ernie Pyle, later killed by a sniper. Newsreels of the war brutalities confirmed the gruesome reports. The Philippines, Bataan and Corregidor were only a few of the places of intense slaughter.

As the war tempo speeded up in the South Pacific in the spring of 1942, the snow drifts in New York began to melt. Trees sprouted into their lush green garb. Tulips stood tall and erect in their red and yellow bonnets. Roses ran riot in deep red or soft pink shades. Nature seemed normal, but nothing else was!

I finished the school term on May 29, but did not sign another teaching contract for fall. I felt so restless and uncertain about what to do next. Should I look for another girl trained in linguistics and go back to Brazil? Or should I serve my country in the war effort?

In June of 1942, my brother Tom enlisted in the Air Force. He was assigned to basic training in Illinois and then went to Texas. From there he was assigned to the Tenth American Air Force and saw action on the African front.

Also in July, a neighbor of ours came home on furlough. He was First Lieutenant John Arnold of the U.S. Army, currently serving in the Intelligence Department in London, England.

John looked quite dashing in his new uniform of olive green trimmed with gold buttons. So my mother thought as she saw him walking into the Arnold home.

On Monday morning while she hung out the weekly wash, she noticed John in his backyard and called to him. "How about having dinner with us tomorrow night? We haven't seen you in ages!"

"Say, that sounds like a swell idea. I'll be there," he answered.

His tall, slim figure with dark, wavy hair and deep brown eyes complemented his classy uniform.

I had known John most of my life. But as he was four years older than I, he finished college before I started. While growing up as neighbor kids, he often teased me and pulled my long blonde braids, which I really detested.

However, the next evening when our doorbell rang, I opened the door. There was John—smiling and looking very handsome with the shiny silver bars on his uniform.

During the dinner hour, I stole a few glances at him. How could anyone change so much? Could an Army uniform alone turn a pest into a prince?

Then he looked at me and said, "I never realized when I grew up here in Fairmont that some day I'd be working in Army Intelligence in London. This war sure has uprooted a lot of us."

"Sounds exciting," I answered. "But isn't it risky to live in London where the German planes have done so much bombing?"

"For sure," he replied. "But no place in Europe seems safe these days."

"What kind of work do you do?" queried my father.

"Well, our department is highly secretive. We do work with the British Intelligence and also the French Resistance. But... hey, I'd better say no more. Classified stuff—you understand."

"Didn't mean to pry," added Dad apologetically.

"I know you didn't, but *we* can't be too careful, either."

And turning to me, he asked, "Didn't you major in languages in college, Ruth?"

"That's right," I replied.

"How many can you handle—with some fluency?"

Hedging a little, I replied, "About five—plus English."

John raised his eyebrows with interest. After a short pause he asked, "Have you considered joining the Women's Army Corps? We could really use a good linguist in our department."

"Well, actually . . . I am very undecided as to what I should do right now. But if there's some way I can help my country, I'm willing to give it a try."

Mother then mentioned our former grade school years . . . about the time John thought he had lost his beloved dog Blackie.

I had always thought of John as being too old for me. And he had just loved to pester me when we were kids. Then after he went off to college, we sort of lost track of each other.

John left our place about 11 o'clock. As I climbed the stairway to my room that evening, I had to admit that he had been quite charming. Had time really changed him for the better?

The next day I wrote to the Mission Board, asking if another single girl trained in linguistics were available to go back with me to Brazil. They wrote that with the war going on and so many ships being sunk in the Atlantic, they would not send out any missionaries to the Amazon at this time.

During the next few weeks I often thought about John's suggestion that I join the Women's Army Corps. But I still grieved over the loss of Steve and didn't feel ready for anything that drastic—yet anyway.

Finally on September 15, 1942, Dad said to me at the breakfast table, "Honey, I just had a letter from my brother Maurice in Seattle. He mentioned that there was a good job opening in their Post Office. In fact, they wanted someone with a background in foreign languages. Sound interesting to you?"

I looked at him and answered, "Say, I believe I'd like a job like that! I'll call him tonight and see what I'd have to do to apply for it."

"Sure don't like to see you go that far away," added Dad, "but I know you want a good job soon."

I phoned Uncle Maurice and he said he would find out more about the position and let me know the details for applying.

With so many young people in the Armed Forces or in war factory jobs, help of any kind was extremely hard to get right now.

Late Friday night Uncle Maurice called and told me to get on a train to Seattle right away. He was quite sure I'd get the job. But first I'd have to take a difficult test there.

That weekend I took care of some business and packed a couple of suitcases.

On Tuesday afternoon I boarded the train for Seattle. While the train steamed through the flat Dakota prairies I wondered if I had acted too quickly. The train was crowded with both soldiers and civilians, but still I felt lonely. And I didn't know anyone in Seattle except my uncle and his family.

While passing through the majestic Rockies, the snow-capped mountains somehow lifted my spirits. Surely, no scenery could match this—any place!

As our train pulled into Seattle, I really hoped Uncle Maurice would be there to meet me. He knew the time of my arrival.

As I stepped down onto the platform, I heard someone say, "Over here, Ruth!"

How good to see his smiling face among all the strangers. Although I hadn't seen my uncle since I was in third grade, we had exchanged family snapshots every Christmas. We didn't travel much when I was young because my father's drugstore business kept him tied down. But we did manage to make that one trip to Seattle when I was eight years old.

"You must be really tired, having been on that train for four days," he added, taking my arm.

"Not too bad," I answered. "But honestly . . . I am glad to be here now."

Then he grabbed my suitcases and led me to his Pontiac in the parking lot. Soon we were driving in heavy traffic, heading for his home on Vine Street.

My Aunt Irene had prepared a delicious dinner that evening of baked salmon. I had never eaten such tasty fish before.

Afterward, we went into their living room to visit. They had so many questions to ask about our family. I just gave them the highlights of the past 18 years.

About midnight Irene said, "Maurice, we mustn't keep her up any longer. We're on Pacific time, so Ruth must be exhausted!"

"Right, my dear," he replied.

Irene then took me up to the guest room on second floor. How good the bed looked! After spending three nights sitting up in a train seat, I could hardly wait to crawl between the clean sheets.

Saturday was spent getting settled in. Some of my dresses needed pressing and I also washed out a few things in their laundry room.

Irene told me that their son Lloyd was in the Navy in the South Pacific and their younger son George had joined the Royal Canadian Air Force.

Sunday morning we all attended church. The service was inspiring and the place was crowded with people.

Later in the afternoon, Maurice drove us around Seattle so I could see the downtown buildings and the shoreline, where there were boats of all kinds. Seattle was fascinating! I was glad I'd come. Now, if I could only land that post office job.

Early on Monday morning, my uncle drove me down to the Post Office. Here I had to fill out a number of forms, plus take a six-page test. It was hard!

By noon I had finished, so got on a bus that stopped near my uncle's home. I waited the rest of that day and all day Tuesday. What would I do if this job didn't materialize? Maurice tried to comfort me by saying there were other jobs available, but they might not be as interesting as the one in the Post Office.

However, on Wednesday the postmaster called and offered me a position in the censorship office, to check on subversive mail, both foreign and local. My knowing five foreign languages really helped me get the job, he said. And this office was now operated by the military.

After a couple of months on this job, I was made the head of the foreign table of readers. It was important to record whatever was of a suspicious nature that could be useful to military operations.

But just when I was feeling at home with the work, the military was called to active overseas duty, and the entire censorship operation was turned over to civilians.

Nevertheless, the months flew by. Then one day in March of 1943, Maurice asked me, "How's the job going?"

"I don't know what to say about it now. I enjoyed the work more when the military was in charge," I replied.

Each day as I rode the bus to work, I became more impressed with the slogans recruiting women for the Army. The posters read: "Women, men are dying on the battle lines. Can you live with yourself on the sidelines?"

In addition, there was some political stuff going on in our office that bothered me. And those posters kept gnawing at my conscience. What should I do?

The following week, I resigned and went down to the Women's Army Auxiliary Corps recruiting center on Pike Street and enlisted.

But that very evening as I walked toward my uncle's home, I heard heavy footsteps behind me. Just as I turned to cross the lawn, a gruff voice demanded, "Give me your purse!"

"I will not!" I shouted and tried to run for the house. But the tall, heavy-set man grabbed my purse and pushed me to the ground.

I screamed loudly, but he took off with my purse and crossed the street into the darkness.

Fortunately, I wasn't hurt but was very frightened. I quickly got to my feet, ran into the house and called the police.

I had had only ten dollars in my purse, but I also lost all my identification papers for joining the WACs.

When my uncle came home, he was very angry about the whole thing. "Be sure you catch that thief!" he shouted to the police, who were now at the house.

At any rate, we were all thankful that I had not been hurt or attacked. At breakfast the next morning, Maurice showed me the *Seattle Intelligencer.* It said: "WAC expects excitement. She finds it." I had made the headlines.

My military orders came a few days later. They were dated May 6, 1943. I was told to report to the 5th Women's Army Auxiliary Corps Training Center at Monticello, Arkansas, on May 10. The thought frightened me. What had I done? Was this really God's plan for me?

Too late to turn back now. As I boarded the train for Monticello with five other girls from Seattle, I discovered that some of them were school librarians and teachers.

That night on the train, I had a nightmare. Probably a result of the purse-snatching episode. In the darkness, I screamed out loud.

The next morning, one of the girls asked, "Who was that screaming last night?"

But I was too ashamed to admit that I was the guilty one! However, before we got to Monticello the train stopped unexpectedly.

The girl seated next to me, whose name was Barbara Williams, asked, "What's going on?"

Captain June Kennedy answered, "Sorry ladies, we are marooned here by flood waters ahead. We'll probably have to wait here for a few days before going on to camp. Maybe I can find some books for you to read to help pass the time of day."

Fortunately, we had plenty to eat on board and I found a copy of the novel *Magnificent Obsession* to read. It was very interesting and kept me from brooding about the layover.

By the third day, the water had gone down so we got to our camp at Monticello. Barbara and I became good friends as we had many common interests.

But for being only May, it was really *hot* in Monticello! The heat was unbearable at night and we couldn't sleep. So we took walks in our robes at night (even against the rules).

I soon discovered that Army life was rugged and I was soft. Early morning reveille, keeping the barracks open for inspection, and marching. When my muscles ached at night, I thought I had taken on more than I could handle.

Next, we were given the opportunity to apply for officer training. They especially encouraged those of us with college degrees. But somehow it didn't appeal to me. I wanted to be with the rank and file.

Back in first grade, my teacher had scolded me for not keeping in step. Now I was in the Army, marching for dear old Uncle Sam. As the girls marched along singing Army songs, I found comfort in quoting Scripture I had memorized as a child.

And one day out of the clear blue sky, this verse flashed into my mind: "Christ in you, the hope of glory." Since then, that verse has become a precious reality, the mystery of the Gospel.

After four tough weeks of basic training, I was assigned to Fort Devens, Massachusetts. At Fort Devens, the Captain said,

"If any of you women do not meet the physical requirements for overseas duty, you will be discharged."

That night I looked at my varicose veins and knew they would not pass me in this condition.

So the next morning I asked Captain Kennedy what I should do.

"Why don't you go to Boston for treatment of your veins," she suggested.

"Will they let me go?" I inquired.

"I'll see that you are given permission," she smiled.

Somehow after coming this far, I really wanted to go overseas. And after the doctors treated me in Boston, I passed the physical test and was assigned to overseas duty.

Training at Fort Devens was exciting. However, because of the time lost in getting those treatments in Boston, I was separated from my first contingent of WACs.

As I walked the long corridor of the new barracks carrying my heavy duffel bag, I prayed, "Lord, help me find a Christian for a bunkmate."

Then on a shelf above one of the beds, I saw a New Testament. Here was my answer—already.

Before I had fully settled in, the owner of the Testament appeared. Her name was Miriam Burk and what a joy to have a person like her for a roommate!

After we had received our overseas assignment, I asked Miriam, "Where do you think they'll send us?"

"No one knows," she answered. "Top-secret."

Garbed in military dress with our green helmets on, we marched in a complete blackout down the long gangplank.

Of course, I had been in the New York harbor several times before, but nothing looked familiar now.

We boarded an unidentified steamer that was already loaded with troops. Our separate quarters were crowded. But soon we moved out to high seas.

At O4OO, Miriam woke me and asked, "Doesn't it sound strange?" (0400 is Army time for 4:00 a.m.)

"Why, what do you mean?" I asked.

"This complete silence is abnormal."

"You're right," I replied. "There's no engine noise now."

"Do you suppose there's a German submarine out there looking for us?" she queried.

"Could be. They probably shut down the engines so the U-boats can't use the sound waves for a sighting," I added.

The moments were tense and each minute seemed like an hour. But finally at 0800, we heard the rumble of the engines kicking in again.

"Where do you think we are headed for?" asked Miriam with concern.

"Have no idea," I replied.

A few minutes later, we were notified that we were approaching Newfoundland and had to disembark because our ship was having boiler problems.

While we waited for another ship to pick us up, we sat on the banks of the St. John River. Here was a place of peace in the midst of a war-torn world.

Finally, another ship did come and took us to Liverpool, England. Fortunately, no submarines attacked our convoy on the entire trip across the Atlantic.

At first we were housed temporarily in a British barracks at Stone, England, to be processed and then sent on to London. Here I was assigned to the SHAEF Message Center of Communications. We were then issued the SHAEF insignia, (SHAEF — Supreme Headquarters, Allied Expeditionary Forces).

On a black background, this insignia showed the flaming sword that would pierce the forces of Nazi power that dominated Europe. Above the sword was a rainbow, symbol of hope, containing all the colors of the national flags of the Allies. G-2 SHAEF was the Intelligence branch for General Eisenhower's headquarters. We WACs were housed at Sloane Court, from which we commuted in Army trucks to the camouflaged Peter Robinson Building in the heart of London. There on the fifth floor was the message center.

After working here about a month, Miriam asked me one day, "What do you think of those German buzz bombs?"

"They're awful!" I answered. "And they cause so much devastation, exploding on London both day and night. Aimed at military installations, they also hit civilian homes and churches."

While we were stationed at Sloane Court, a group of GIs were living in the adjoining court.

Then it happened . . . one day at 0500. A direct hit on us by a German bomber!

As the walls around me collapsed, I fell to my knees and prayed. Miriam cried out, "Ruth, Ruth! Where are you? They really got us this time, didn't they?"

"Over here," I answered. "Are you hurt?"

"Don't think so," she replied, "but perhaps I'm just numb from fright."

"Wait a minute! Listen!" I shouted. "Do you hear those awful cries for help? Must be from the soldier sleeping in the next court."

"Won't somebody please come and help them?" pleaded Miriam.

"We can't, 'cause we're almost buried in this debris ourselves," I answered.

It took several hours for help to arrive. This seemed like forever to us, who were trying to breathe in the collapsed room.

Heavy equipment finally came to remove the broken walls and collapsed roofs.

After they got some of the ruins hauled away, I could see the sun. It never looked so good!

Miriam asked one of the helpers, "Did the soldiers in the other court get out okay?"

He just shook his head sadly. After taking a deep breath, he added, "Sorry, lady . . . none of them survived the bombing."

We all broke down and cried aloud. Why had death passed over the women and taken all the men? What did it all mean?

After dusting off our uniforms, we walked away. And all of us WACs reported for work that day. No one was even injured, but mighty shook up, I'd say.

Captain Gene Staley now had to assign us to temporary quarters. Miriam and I were to stay at the Lucas Ashley home not far from the Robinson Building. The others went to an apartment complex or other private homes in the area.

What would it be like to live with a family of complete strangers? I wondered.

Chapter 8

The Challenge

"You gals were sure lucky to have lived through that direct hit on Sloane Court yesterday!" exclaimed John Arnold, as he breezed into my office the following day.

I could hardly believe my eyes. Here was my next-door neighbor from Fairmont now working in the same building as I. Only he was on a different floor. It took a while to regain my composure. Then I said, "If only those poor GIs had gotten out alive, too."

John looked down sadly, but went on to ask, "By the way, where are you staying now?"

"Miriam and I are most fortunate in being assigned to temporary quarters at the Ashleys. They are a dear, retired couple with a lovely home. Even have a cute white shaggy dog!"

At that moment Colonel Clark walked briskly into my room. After the customary salutes, he asked John, "Will you come into my office for a few minutes?"

John immediately followed the Colonel into his private quarters down on second floor. Clark then said, "Sit down, John . . . at ease."

John pulled a sturdy brown chair toward the Colonel's desk and sat in it.

Clark leaned his elbow on the massive desk and looked intently at John.

"I've been watching your work closely," he stated. "Would you be interested in doing a special assignment? It's highly risky, but if anyone can get the job done, you can."

"Well, well . . . thank you, Sir," stammered John, quite surprised at the unexpected compliment. "Just what did you have in mind?"

"As you know, we are getting lots of material from Ultra—the British code breaking center. They help us find out what the old Krauts are planning next. Anyway, we'd like you to work with the French Forces of the Interior and Underground Resistance."

John now sat erect in rapt attention.

Clark cleared his throat. "From their command post, a few Frenchmen will go with you on some secret missions."

"Doing what?" queried John.

"All sorts of things—like intercepting radio conversations, questioning prisoners, checking the bodies of dead soldiers for letters or battle plans . . . whatever."

"Whew!"

"Rumor has it that the Germans are working on some secret weapons and also a high-powered rocket engine. We need some real data on that business right away!"

John's eyes opened widely and he whistled softly. "Man, that's exciting but plenty dangerous, I'll bet!"

"You can say that again. That's why you'd better think it over carefully for a few days before giving me your decision. Don't discuss this with anyone, though—understand?"

"I do, Sir. Appreciate your considering me. Perhaps I can give you my answer sometime tomorrow."

"Good!" answered Clark, as his face broke into a broad grin. After saluting each other, John left the Colonel's office.

In his own quarters that night, John slept fitfully, He kept weighing the risk factor against the intrigue and importance of these missions for his country—and perhaps the world!

War is always hazardous, he mused. In his favor, John was still single with no family responsibilities. Would the risk be worth the possible gain? Well, at any rate, he decided to accept the challenge.

At 0800 the following morning, John hurried to the Colonel's office.

"Go right in," said Clark's secretary. "He's expecting you."

John smiled at her and walked through the larger office, then opened the door into a smaller, private room.

After the usual saluting, John said, "I've thought it over, Sir, and decided to accept."

"Good boy!" exclaimed the Colonel, as he slapped John warmly on the shoulder. "Now, go back and pack your duffel bag. At noon I'll have Sergeant Smythe drive you to the first station of your journey. We'll be getting some help from the French Underground on your way to de Gaulle's temporary quarters."

"Yes, Sir."

The two officers shook hands and parted.

Promptly at noon, Smythe's jeep squealed to a halt in front of John's quarters. John hurried out and tossed his heavy bag into the back of the vehicle. Then he slid into the seat next to the driver.

"Gonna be a tiresome, bumpy ride ahead. These jeeps are long on dependability, but short on comfort," drawled Smythe nonchalantly.

The jeep jostled over the green and amber English countryside. The rolling hills and fields of grain were a marked contrast to the noise and rubble in populous London.

John looked over at his partner and said, "Sometime, when this crazy war is over, I'd like to return and just leisurely tour dear old England."

"Nice thought," sighed the Sergeant. "Only hope those blasted Krauts don't bomb merry old England right off the map!"

Several hours later the jeep stopped at a small seaport on the southeastern coast of Britain. Smythe pointed to a sleek white and gold yacht in the harbor. "There's your boat, Sir. It'll take you to the French coast."

"Thanks, pal," added John.

After climbing out of the jeep, John tossed his duffel bag over his shoulder and boarded the fancy vessel. The skipper, dressed in a white uniform with gold braid, greeted John and handed him a large brown envelope with sealed instructions inside. John went off by himself and opened it.

The yacht then headed east for a small harbor south of St. Malo, France. The letter in the envelope told John to make contact with a gentleman wearing a long, gray coat and matching hat, with a purple feather in its brim.

While the boat was in the middle of the English Channel, John began having some real doubts. What was he getting into? But he had made the fateful decision himself—and it was too late to turn back now.

Fortunately, the weather was pleasant for sailing and soon he sighted the French shoreline. He began looking for a man dressed in gray, but there wasn't a single person on land.

The yacht pulled up to the dock and John jumped off with his duffel bag. He waved to the skipper and began walking along the well-worn platform. Had there been a slip-up somewhere?

The skipper had not identified himself or even spoken with John during the entire trip across. And now the yacht turned around quickly and sped back toward England.

Alone on the shore of a strange country, John felt forsaken. What if no one came to meet him? And France was now enemy territory, being occupied by the Nazis! What should he do?

As he sat on his duffel bag, John searched up and down the coastline. Fifteen long minutes passed. They seemed like an eternity.

Finally he saw a black car drive up and stop. John held his breath. Was it friend or foe?

The man climbing out of the car was dressed in gray and had a purple feather in his hat brim. *This must be the contact man,* he thought.

The Frenchman looked around and seeing no one else came toward John. Then he whispered, "Are you Lieutenant Arnold?"

"I am."

"Come with me, then. You are to stay in my home tonight. In the morning I'll tell you the plans for the day."

John got into the old black car. He wondered what lay ahead now.

"Hard for me to get used to seeing you people drive on the left side of the road," said John, trying to make conversation.

"By Jove," laughed the Frenchman, "I suppose it is different for you Yanks. But you young fellows seem to catch on to things rather quickly."

After going about a mile east, they came to a spacious beige and brown house at the edge of town.

A narrow river curled through the backyard of this property. A beautiful row of tall spruce trees made a natural private boundary on the north—between the beige house and the nearest neighbor.

The Frenchman never told John who he was or what he did for a living. And John never asked. The Nazis had occupied France for the past three years, but most of the smaller towns were left pretty much alone. Their large occupational forces were mostly in the densely populated cities.

That evening John's host prepared a simple meal of fried fish, bread and creamed cabbage.

"Sorry, old chap," he said to John, "wish I could serve a better fare, but food is hard to come by these days."

"Don't apologize. It tastes great!" exclaimed John.

"I'm so tired of eating cabbage, but the Nazis take our best food for their own use.

"I can believe that," replied John. "And I sure do appreciate your sharing your house and food with me. Must take a lot of scrounging for food—just to keep alive."

"Can't wait till this old war gets over with and things get back to normal," said the Frenchman. "By the way, I'm originally from England. Should have stayed there, but came over here some years ago for business reasons."

After the wood in the fireplace sputtered and died out, the host showed John to his upstairs bedroom. The beautiful mahogany furniture, white chenille bedspread and lace curtains reminded John of his parents' home in Fairmont.

After crawling into bed, he wondered, *What are the folks doing right now? Will I ever see them alive again?*

With all these conflicting thoughts revolving around in his head, it took several hours before he finally fell asleep.

The new morning arrived with a clear, sunny sky. A group of birds outside his window formed a chirping choir. Perhaps they were trying to cheer up the discouraged French people.

After dressing and shaving, John sat down with his nameless host at the breakfast table. It was a simple meal of oatmeal and coffee, plus toast.

"Today you won't be going anywhere," stated the Frenchman rather sternly. The frown on his dark bushy eyebrows added to the grimness of his words. "But tonight, a friend of mine will escort you to the next underground station."

John had heard rumors about the workings of the French Underground since France had come under the control of the Nazis. Now he would learn firsthand how effective their secret organization really was.

His host added, "Better get extra rest during the day, too. Incidentally, there are lots of books in my library—in case you're interested in reading. I'll be at my office as usual, but will join you this evening for dinner."

"Can't thank you enough for all this," replied John as he extended his hand in gratitude.

"Remember . . . don't leave this house at any time today! We never know when someone will betray a friend or enemy for some bribe money from the Germans."

"Will do. Sure appreciate that you're willing to risk your life to help me on my journey."

"I'll do almost anything for the Underground. Hope we can soon get rid of those lousy Nazi invaders. Jolly glad you Yanks finally came over to help us."

"Who would ever have thought that Germany would try the second time to rule the world?" asked John as he remembered World War I.

"Isn't that the truth!" agreed the Frenchman. "And we were so totally unprepared for their surprise attack. And now we are paying dearly for it. Sometimes I wake up at night and think it's just a bad nightmare. But then reality hits! With rationing, betrayal and war reports on the radio."

He shook his head in despair and then quietly left for his office.

John remained in the comfortable beige house all that day. The hours passed by slowly for John before his host returned and they again shared dinner together.

At 2200 (ten o'clock) that evening, there was a coded knock at the door. The Frenchman answered it.

"Come in quickly," he whispered. After the stranger removed his cap, the host continued. "This is our American friend. Take him at once to Station Four. From there someone else will escort him further."

"Good," answered the short, dark-haired man, dressed in dark green clothing and wearing a black beret on his head. "Hey, Yank, let's get started! Gotta be back here before dawn comes, ya know."

He was one of the Maquis, the French resistance fighters. They often hid in the forests by day and blew up trains and bridges by night.

John grabbed his duffel bag and the two men quietly slipped out of the house. A bright moon gave them some help in finding their way in the darkness. But it also meant extra caution—like not walking in open fields. Instead, they carefully followed the fence lines or edges of the woods.

After trudging along silently until 1300 hours, they suddenly noticed a very bright light moving in the distance beyond.

The member of the Maquis whispered to John, "Stop. That might be a Nazi guard on night patrol. We're near a large city."

The men crept toward two bushy evergreen trees growing side by side. Now crouched behind the trees, they did not talk or move.

In the moonlight John saw two figures coming right toward them. One was holding a spotlight in his right hand.

John and his escort remained motionless behind the two big trees. As the two silhouettes came nearer, John noticed that both were dressed in military uniforms.

They scarcely breathed. When the two Nazis were within twenty feet of the protecting trees, the one with the searchlight paused a minute. It was painfully still and each second seemed like a year.

At last the Nazi soldier laughed nervously and motioned to his partner to move on toward the city.

John and his colleague remained silent behind the trees for another 15 minutes before proceeding on their journey.

"That was awfully close," groaned John. "Do you suppose they had been tipped off about our coming? Or was this just a routine night patrol?"

"Who knows?" answered the man in the black beret. "Lots of spy work going on with both sides in this crazy war. Sure glad they didn't find us. Would have been torture or death—if we'd been caught!"

"Yeah, I can believe that," sighed John.

"Come on, Yank, hurry up! I've simply got to get back home before sunrise."

The two men walked on faster and by 1400 hours, they reached Station Four. It was an old barn on a farm only five miles from the city of Argentan.

The Maquis member rapped his coded knock on the sagging barn door. Several minutes later, a lady about 40 years old opened the door cautiously.

"Come in, come in," she whispered.

"This is our American friend," said the escort. "Now I simply must leave here at once."

As he departed, the French lady looked at John and pointed up to the hayloft. She had soft brown eyes, olive complexion and her black hair was parted in the middle.

She said, "If you climb that ladder to the loft, you'll find a tiny storeroom up there with some bedding in it. Try to get some sleep. I'll bring you food in the morning. Au revoir."

John just nodded his head in appreciation, feeling very tired right now. He then walked toward the old wooden ladder. It looked rather weak, but he hoped it would be strong enough for him to climb up to the loft.

The petite French woman quietly closed the barn door behind her and strolled slowly toward her house.

John lay down on some old quilts and thought about the efficiency of the Underground Movement. Being exhausted, however, he soon drifted off into an uneasy sleep.

Just before daybreak he awoke with a start at the sound of a strange, piercing noise. Sitting up at once, he looked carefully around.

"Fooey—just an old rooster," he muttered to himself when he realized what had made the shrill noise. "Bet that old bird doesn't even know there is some fighting going on—and maybe not far away either."

About 0700 in the morning, the farm lady cautiously opened the aged barn door. Under a white cloth, she carried a tray with pancakes and coffee for John.

The pleasing aroma of hot coffee made John climb quickly down the weak ladder. She then handed him an old three-legged milk stool on which to sit. Smiling sweetly she said, "Sorry I don't have any sausage to give you with the cakes. But meat is about impossible to come by these days."

"That's okay; these pancakes will do just fine."

"Stay in the barn all day," she whispered to him as though the walls had ears. "I'll bring your meals here."

"Thanks, lady."

"Tonight someone from the Resistance Army will come and take you to their command post."

Scratching his head, John asked her, "Why do you people in the Underground take all these chances? The risks are high, you know."

"Yes they are. But we'll do almost anything we can to help the Allies. The German soldiers have been so cruel to the French. Why . . . only two years ago they gunned down my dear husband. And for no reason at all!"

"I'm so sorry," added John.

Taking a deep breath she continued, "Every day we dream of the wonderful hour of liberation when France and the other countries will be rid of this awful Nazi scourge!"

John looked at her with pity, then added, "I'll be careful and stay out of sight today."

Suddenly she turned around and left the barn. Through the window near the door, he noticed her two-story stone farm house. Inconspicuous, but now being very useful to the Underground — and him!

After hurriedly eating the pancakes, John strolled over to one of the milk cows standing in another part of the large barn. He had always had a tender feeling for animals and this particular black and white Holstein appreciated the petting.

As the day dragged on, John experienced a feeling of claustraphobia from being cooped up in the smelly old building.

"Oh for a nice walk in the clean country air," he said to the cow which looked at him and mooed.

Then he was startled by another noise. He looked around quickly to see what it was, but decided he'd heard only the rain beginning to splash against the tiled roof. *Nice to be inside now,* he mused.

Later on he climbed up into the hayloft, letting the drip, drip of the rain lull him to sleep.

As he rested he thought about all the GIs at various battle fronts. How could they endure the rainy, cold weather and live in foxholes for months at a time? Perhaps he'd soon find out for himself!

After waking up in the late afternoon, John noticed an old tin cup in one of the window sills. He grabbed it, opened the window a few inches, and held the cup outside. The steady rain rinsed it out somewhat.

Then picking up the milk stool, he placed it beneath the friendly bossy he had petted earlier and sat down. In a few minutes, he had pulled down a nice cup of thick, fresh milk. Smacking his lips, he thought, *This would have tasted better cold, but at least it is real milk.*

Around sunset the barn door again creaked open. The kind French woman, now dressed in a pretty navy blue dress with a white lace collar, entered quietly with his dinner on a tray. She did not stay and talk, but left the food and walked back to her home.

The meal was simple, but tasty. An improvement over the monotonous GI rations, at any rate. But he really hoped she hadn't given him too much of her own meager food supply.

At 2100 hours in the evening came the classic knock on the barn door. John peeked through a small crack in it, then opened the door cautiously.

In the semi-darkness, he saw the French Resistance fighter and shook hands with him.

"I'm Sergeant Raynaud from our secret headquarters," he said. "And you must be Lieutenant John Arnold from London."

"Right, friend! Glad to meet you, Sergeant."

"Then let's be on our way. No time to waste."

Quietly the two soldiers slipped away from the aged barn, now badly in need of paint and repair. The darkness felt heavy.

They walked by the edge of a thick forest. John's duffel bag felt heavier by the hour. He was definitely glad that this would be his last night of travel on this trip. Often a branch would slap across his face as they stumbled along in the dark, windy night.

While they trudged over the bumpy terrain, the yellow moon gave them a little light, even though some whispy blue clouds often floated past the bright moon.

Just before dawn broke through on the eastern horizon, the Sergeant said, "Hang in there, old Yank. We're almost home now."

"Home" proved to be a rather sprawling, hip-roofed barn. Surrounding it was a vast open field, full of olive green tents. The place looked like a "no man's land" . . . probably why it had been chosen for the Resistance command post. The enemy would scarcely look for an important post way out in this wilderness.

Sergeant Raynaud led John directly into the inner office, that of General Charles de Gaulle himself.

What John would experience in the days to come, he never in his wildest imagination could have foreseen!

Chapter 9

High Risk Factor

John crisply saluted the General.

As de Gaulle extended his large, bony hand, he said, "Glad to see you, Lieutenant Arnold."

"Thank you, Sir. Wouldn't have made it here without the help of the Underground, though."

"Absolutely right. As you might know, I have headquarters for the Free French in London and also in Africa, but once in a while I fly over here to see how the Resistance fighters are doing. And right now, Ultra tells us that the Germans are working on a couple of new, powerful weapons. And . . . should these get perfected and put into operation soon, it might mean we lose the big war!"

John whistled softly. "That serious?"

"Definitely! And our pressing priority is to find out what kind of weapons they are and where they are being made."

"I see."

"This is where you come in, Arnold. We want you to work closely with a group of men from here—to search everywhere for that data."

"Meaning?"

"Try all ways possible to learn about them—such as intercepting radio messages, hunting for battle plans and letters on dead bodies. Anything . . . that might give us the missing pieces to this weapons puzzle."

"Hmm . . . this sounds both important and dangerous!" added John.

"That's putting it mildly," answered the General. Then he sat down on an old chair.

John waited for de Gaulle to continue.

Looking sternly into John's eyes, he added, "You'll meet Captain LeBeau this evening. Then tomorrow he and the others, and you, will head for the battle front. LeBeau can answer any questions you might have."

"Yes, Sir."

"Better get some rest now. You'll need a clear head for this big undertaking."

As John left the office, he wondered where to go. But suddenly a young soldier walked toward him.

"I'm Corporal Holloway," he stated. "You must be Lieutenant Arnold. Come with me and I'll show you where you'll be bunking tonight."

He led John to a large tent containing eight cots. "Take your choice of one of the three empty ones," said the Corporal.

John took the one nearest the entrance and gladly tossed down his heavy duffel bag. Tired, he sat down and was thankful he had made the trip safely—so far, anyway.

"There is breakfast at 0500 in the mess hall," added Holloway. "After that a van will take your group to where the action is. Until then you are free to rest, read or write letters. Good luck, Sir."

They saluted each other and John was left alone.

Some months before this, John had received special training to become an Ultra representative. He learned how to interpret the raw data of German messages. Now he would be part of an Ultra team, traveling with top secret baggage, radios, encoding and decoding machines, files and so on. Two military policemen, as guards, went with each special van.

Just before he retired for the night, Captain LeBeau entered John's tent and introduced himself.

"Glad to meet you, Sir," replied John.

"We have a big day ahead of us tomorrow, so I won't stay long," said LeBeau. "But I do want to say I'm glad you made it here safely and are willing to work with us."

"My privilege," added John.

After a hearty breakfast the next morning, John walked over to Captain LeBeau whom he had met briefly the night before. LeBeau then introduced John to Lieutenant Dwyer and the two guards, Ray and Jerry. After getting into the brown van, the soldiers headed east.

They drove for about 30 minutes before Captain LeBeau asked Ray to pull off the road and stop behind a small grove of trees. He then raised a couple of antennas and soon heard German-speaking voices over the radio.

"Quiet, men," he ordered. "I think I'm picking up a Nazi patrol talking with their command post.

Arnold and Dwyer huddled close to LeBeau to hear what was being said. They jotted down some notes, as they all understood the German language.

The Nazis conversed for ten minutes, then abruptly stopped. The group finished writing their notes and put them into a large manila envelope. Captain LeBeau then hid this envelope under the floor mat of the van.

LeBeau continued, "Ray, back up a ways and head north on that graveled road."

After angling northeast about eight more miles, the van again pulled off the road. Ray parked it behind a small hill.

LeBeau ordered, "Ray, stay here with the van. The rest of us will go on ahead."

From the radio message, the group had learned that not far from where they were now, a German platoon had been almost annihilated in fierce combat. And their medical corps personnel would not be able to care for the dead or wounded for another four hours.

"This will be a gory affair, but we'll have a chance to look for important papers or letters that the soldiers might have carried on themselves. The surprise attack sure caught the old Krauts off guard!" exclaimed LeBeau.

The four Allies kept close to the ground, slowly making their way around a dense thicket. Would they walk into a trap? The enemy had often given out false information to trick the Allies, too.

Suddenly, the horrible battle scene was before them. They gasped. Mutilated bodies . . . bloody clothing . . . heaps of dirt mixed with flesh. Above all, the nauseating smell of gunpowder and decaying bodies.

"Man, oh man, I can't believe what we're seeing!" exclaimed LeBeau. Then, clearing his throat, he tried to gain control of himself.

"Look at their uniforms," added the Captain. "Search the officers first and then anything else that might look suspicious."

John found it difficult to move or think. But he forced himself to examine the remains of a former handsome Nazi general. Soon he discovered some papers neatly sewn into the inner lining of the jacket. But while removing them, a picture also fell to the ground. As he picked it up he noticed that it was the photo of an attractive blonde woman and her two robust children. Probably the general's wife and sons, he thought.

"What a waste and sorrow this war is," said John to Captain LeBeau. Then he showed him the picture.

LeBeau glanced at the photo and shook his head. John then put it in with the papers he had taken from the clothing of the corpse.

The four soldiers continued searching among the victims. Time was crucial. They found several letters and other documents.

Jerry was supposed to be on lookout, but he couldn't resist taking a Luger from one of the bodies. He slipped this gun into his pocket as a souvenir of the awful war.

In a short time the sight and smell of blood and flesh became unbearable, so LeBeau shouted, "Hey, men, let's head for the van and hurry home!"

Finally, thought John to himself. But he couldn't forget the grief that would soon come to the families of the fallen soldiers.

When Ray saw his friends coming around the bend in the trail, he put the key into the ignition. All of them were most anxious to leave this eerie place as soon as possible.

John glanced over his shoulder several times. There was always the possibility of another German patrol coming up over the hill—using them for target practice!

Ray laid a patch of rubber on the graveled road and didn't slow down until they reached their command post. Although it was now time for the evening meal, none of them went to the mess hall. What they had just experienced was too much for their stomachs.

"Wonder if any of the stuff we found today will be of value to the Allies?" John asked the Captain as they walked toward their tents.

"Who knows?" answered LeBeau. "But at least our part of the mission was a success."

"And we all made it back alive," added John.

Chapter 10

A Surprising Discovery

John and his search party went on three more missions in France before he returned to London. Ultra in Britain continued to feed the American Intelligence Department reams of raw data about German strategy.

All of us in the Robinson Building kept working long hours on our highly classified jobs.

The day of his return, John Arnold came into my office about noon. "Hi, there!" he exclaimed, "Sure glad to be back in civilization for a while at least."

"Nice to see you again," I smiled at him. "But I still can hardly believe that the two of us from Fairmont should meet here in the Robinson Building during wartime."

"Guess miracles do happen—once in a while anyway. By the way, what about us getting together for dinner or something before I have to leave again?" he asked as his brown eyes twinkled.

"Great idea!"

"All rightie, then. How about Sunday at 1300 hours? I know of a fine little restaurant on London's west side."

"I'll be ready," I replied.

Meanwhile, the war with Italy was going better for the Allies. American casualties had been high, but with the increasing victories, several generals were sent back to the European Theater of Operations. Among those was General Eisenhower, who returned to London.

After leaving my office, John drove to Eisenhower's quarters. He brought along the large manila envelope with all the notes, papers and letters that they had gathered in France.

The General looked tired, but grinned at John and said, "Have a chair, my friend, and let's see what you have in that envelope."

After John handed him the material, he motioned for John to sit in one of the comfortable overstuffed chairs.

"Looks interesting, Lieutenant. Good work on that tough assignment. And, by the way, I'm sure glad you got back here safely!"

"Thank you, Sir. So am I."

"You may leave now while I go over these papers more carefully."

Alone at his desk now, Eisenhower slowly checked over the material. Then he got up from his swivel chair, hurried outside and got an aide to drive him to the Robinson Building.

As he entered my office, he teased, "You lucky girl! Here's some top priority stuff that needs to be translated at once."

"Yes, sir," I answered. "I'll get at it this minute."

He grinned at me and then went down to second floor to see Colonel Clark.

I could hardly believe that the famous General Eisenhower was just in my office. But now I had to concentrate on the important work before me.

So I emptied the contents of the large manila envelope onto my desk. As I tried to sort out the material to make the job easier, the photo of the Nazi General's family slid out and fell to the floor.

Carefully I picked it up and looked at the pretty lady and her chubby little boys. While I gazed at those people, I couldn't help feeling sad about all the families being fractured by the terrible war. However, I needed to brush aside these thoughts and get down to business. All the papers and letters were written in German. Some of the information we had already learned through Ultra, but there was also much new material.

For some strange reason, I became intrigued by the picture. It seemed so personal and innocent, but perhaps this was intended as a disguise. Anyhow, I put it aside and hurried on with the translations.

Several hours later with all that completed, I jumped up from my desk, grabbed the photo and walked down to the basement where Lieutenant Marshall's chemical laboratory was.

The door being open, I walked in and said to Marshall, "I may be on the wrong track, but let's test the back of this picture for the possibility of some invisible writing on it."

The tall, handsome officer raised his dark eyebrows and wrinkled his nose, but politely answered, "Okay. Suppose we can give it a try."

He then walked over to the glass cabinets and removed several bottles of different chemicals from them. Putting the contents of three of them together in a beaker, he stirred the solution. Then he brushed this across the back of the photo.

"See anything yet?" I asked anxiously.

"Not a thing," he replied nonchantly. "But wait a second! Let me test it with another chemical that's new on the market—in fact, it's made by a well-known German chemical company."

We waited impatiently, looking intently at the back side of the picture.

Now I began to feel foolish about even bringing it to the lab—especially since Marshall was more than busy with his routine work.

But suddenly he clapped his hands and exclaimed, "Boy, oh boy! Take a look at this. There is some writing appearing on the back of this thing."

"Are you sure?" I asked.

"Yup . . . looks like some tiny German script. Do you want to take this magnifying glass back to your desk to help you decipher the message written there?"

"Will do. At once!"

I practically flew up the stairway to my office. Because of the extremely small writing, it took me almost an hour to get the full content figured out and translated into English.

Just as I finished, Lieutenant Marshall came bounding into my room. "Hey, let's both take this stuff to the General right away!" he exclaimed.

But first, I called Eisenhower's secretary to find out if he were available. He was.

We got into a jeep and hurried to his quarters, the former Commodore Hotel.

His secretary told us to go right into the inner office. I told the General about the message we discovered on the back of the picture in invisible writing and also handed him the large manila envelope with the papers and translations inside.

Eisenhower immediately read the message which had appeared on the back of the photo.

Then after a low whistle, he said, "This is simply great! It tells us about the new German secret weapons . . . the V-1 and V-2 missiles . . . and their formulae. For months we've been trying to get this data. Marvelous job—you two! And we can't forget John Arnold who brought all this stuff back from France."

"Never underestimate a woman's intuition," teased Marshall as he winked at the General.

"But remember now," warned Eisenhower, "don't either of you breathe a word about all this to anyone—here or elsewhere! The enemy must not know we have this vital information."

"You can count on us," answered Marshall.

I nodded in agreement.

We then took the jeep back to the Robinson Building. After we entered it, I heard him whistling as he strolled back to his laboratory. It was the popular song, "Don't Sit Under the Apple Tree With Anyone Else But Me."

I smiled as I climbed the many stairs to my office on fifth floor. From my window I looked out over the busy street. What would this discovery mean for the Allies? What further events lay ahead of us before this terrible war came to an end... or would we ever really win it?

Chapter 11

The Promotion

About a month after our discovery about the missiles, John Arnold returned from another of his secret journeys and stopped by to chat.

"Mornin', my dear," was his cheerful greeting.

"And isn't it nice to see the sun shining after a whole week of low-hanging clouds and drippy weather?" I replied.

"To be sure. By the way, how do you like living in dear old London?" he asked.

"Well . . . I believe they have even more liquid sunshine here than in Seattle. But in spite of all the air raids and blackouts, I'm learning to like it."

"Good. And now . . . how about having dinner with me tonight? You know what happens to people who work too much without any relaxation?"

I smiled, while his eyes danced with mischief.

Then he cleared his throat and added, "I've got a special reason to celebrate today, too."

"And what is that?"

"Just received my promotion. You are now looking at Captain John Arnold!"

Being both pleased and surprised, I answered, "Congratulations! You deserve it, and I would love to celebrate with you."

"Fine. I'll pick you up at the Ashleys' home at the 1900 hour.

After he left, I got busy with the stack of work that was heaped on my desk. There was so much to do, I ate only a sandwich for lunch and kept on typing. When the clock said 1700, I was tired and hurried home.

John arrived promptly and knocked at the door. I let him in and grabbed my purse.

After leaving the house we climbed into the jeep that he had borrowed from the car pool. Good thing I had put on my green pleated skirt because it was no small step to climb into a jeep.

John drove toward a nice eating place in West London. Then he exclaimed, "It'll sure be a treat to get away from army food for one evening! Sometimes no matter what the cooks prepare, it all tastes like goulash."

I knew what he meant although the army food was often better than what some of the civilians had. The Londoners usually had to scrounge around to get enough food to keep going—no luxuries these days.

As this was only my second date since losing Steve, I still had some nagging doubts. Steve had been so . . . so special. However, John had been our neighbor in Fairmont, so I did feel more comfortable with him than anyone else I'd met as yet.

As we drove through the heavy traffic, I said, "My job with American Intelligence is so different from teaching languages at Lincoln High. But I wouldn't have missed this experience for anything!"

"I was glad when I heard you had joined the WACs, but never dreamed we'd both meet here in London," he said.

"Can't forget how surprised and delighted I was the first time you walked into my office," I added.

"Wonder how much longer the war will last?" he asked. "The casualty lists seem to grow longer every passing day and my current assignment is most dangerous."

"This fight for freedom is so costly," I said. "Not only in deaths and injuries, but also in lower moral standards."

"True enough. The temptations of liquor and loose women has been too much for many soldiers and sailors, I fear," he added.

"What do you suppose our country will be like after the war?" I queried.

John just shook his head.

The world had seemingly gone mad. How could Hitler have caused so much suffering and destruction? And the Japanese brutality in the South Pacific—just awful!

Then he looked at me and said, "Hey, this is the time for celebrating my promotion, so let's talk about the good old days in quiet little Fairmont."

The food wasn't so great, but John was delightful company. And I really needed this interlude.

Later in the evening as our jeep jostled home over the rough streets, John turned to me and said, "You lucky girl—getting to live with the Ashleys. When I'm in France, we often have to sleep in muddy foxholes, so I'm more than happy to get back to London."

"Don't know how long I'll be here, but after Sloane Court was bombed out, several of us WACs were sent to private homes."

After we came into the Ashley driveway, John walked with me to the door, gave me a friendly pinch on my cheek, and said, "Good night, Kitten."

For some reason I couldn't quite explain, I felt a little let down as I saw him zoom off into the bright moonlight.

Even at work the next day, I found it rather difficult to concentrate on my reports. We had had such a fun evening! John could be so witty and charming when he wanted to. Made me forget about the terrible war, at least for a while. But would I ever get over losing Steve? The evening hours were always the most lonely.

Only a week after our "promotion celebration," John again left on one of his mysterious trips to France. Would one of these dangerous missions be his last? However, with the frequent bombings of London and other English cities, all of us were walking on thin ice!

The following evening after I had gone to my room, Jane Ashley knocked at my door.

"May I come in?" she asked softly.

"Of course."

"What are you reading, dear?" she asked.

"Letters from my family," I answered.

"Mail is so wonderful when you are far from home. Right? We never had any children, so having you and Miriam with us these past weeks has been a real treat."

"And a blessing for us, I assure you," I said.

Then I reached into my dresser drawer and pulled out a letter.

"Would you like me to read you a few lines from a letter I received from a Marine I used to know in high school?"

"That'd be interesting," replied Jane.

"He wrote this back in January of 1943, when he faced some terrible fighting on Guadalcanal in the South Pacific.

"He said, 'At night when I crawl into my foxhole, I feel as though I haven't the strength to go through another day, but I keep praying and the Lord seems to hold true to His promise—As thy days, so shall thy strength be.'"

Jane wiped some tears from her eyes while I read more of his letter.

She then added, "We'll never really understand how much some of these boys are going through, fighting for freedom. Hopefully, we will eventually win this old war."

"How true. And think of the many soldiers—and civilians—who have already been tortured or killed since 1939," I added.

"I don't dare think about that," she sighed.

After Jane left, I prayed that some day she and Lucas would find new spiritual life in Christ. They were such precious people.

The night was short and morning came too quickly. At my office I found a note from General Eisenhower saying, "Will you translate this strange letter that was accidentally found by one of the soldiers near the Eastern front? It may not be important, but we often get clues from the least likely sources."

The letter was written in low German and quite readable. The author was a Nazi officer. He had written it to his wife in Hamburg, but this letter would never reach her.

After writing about some family matters, the officer casually mentioned the locations of the erection of several launching ramps for the V-1 and V-2 missiles in France.

When finished, I brought the original letter and its translation over to his office in person.

As the General read about the location of the ramps, he said, "This is great! Now we can send our reconnaissance planes over these areas and pin-point their sites. This data is of tremendous importance right now and we must bomb out those launching ramps at once!"

As the days went by, I became more and more impressed with Eisenhower's administrative and military genius. But I often noticed how his sad, tired eyes revealed the burden of all the responsibilities resting on his broad shoulders. The precious lives of millions of fine young men, including his own son!

After a visit to Germany in the 1930s, Charles Lindbergh had reported to our Congress that the German Third Reich had begun a massive buildup of airplanes, tanks, and submarines. No one believed him. But that was the decade of the Great Depression, when America and the rest of the world lived in ignorant complacency.

When Adolph Hitler came into power, the German economy was in bad shape. However, with the war preparations it improved greatly. He also reorganized the school system, placing priority on math, science, aviation and medicine. Even German medical research was almost eight years ahead of ours in the States. And their military equipment was far advanced and in abundant supply.

While the Third Reich was grooming the young Nazi generation for their coming role in world domination, they succeeded in keeping it a secret from the rest of the nations. German factories ran day and night, producing modern airplanes, tanks, ships and U-boats.

And now a recent report from Ultra indicated that their scientists were working on a new high-speed rocket engine for their planes!

Meanwhile in London, I spent most of my evenings with the Ashleys. The four of us often played games, read or just chatted. But every evening at the 2200 hour, we huddled around the radio, listening to the BBC newscasts.

The Ashleys also had a pet dog, Duchess, who was remarkable. I enjoyed throwing a blue rubber ball high into the air. She then leaped up and caught it in her mouth—and seldom missed. When Lucas sat in his special chair, Duchess went into their bedroom, brought out his slippers and laid them at his feet.

Therefore, in spite of the frequent bombings, we did have some happy times together.

But Lucas often remarked, "How much longer can England endure these raids and still be able to function? Will this nightmare ever end?"

Lucas and Jane had always lived without any apparent need of God in their lives. But this present war was very unnerving. Several of their friends had been killed during the air raids. Now Lucas began to wonder what would happen if he or Jane died. Was there a hereafter?

One evening by the fireside, while we enjoyed a second cup of tea, Jane asked me, "How come you read your Bible so often?"

"Well . . . until I was 14, I thought it was a very dry book," I replied.

"Then?"

"At a youth rally I heard a Bible teacher speak on the verse, John 1:12, 'But as many as received Him, to them gave He power to become the sons of God, even to them that believe on His name.'"

Jane looked puzzled.

I went on, "That night the Holy Spirit revealed to me that I was a lost sinner."

"Meaning?"

"Although everyone is born into this world a sinner since the fall of Adam, God provided a solution to our sin problem—His Son, Jesus Christ. I then confessed my sins to the Lord, trusted that this Jesus had died on the cross for my sins and accepted His promise of eternal life. I committed my entire life to Him that night."

"Did this—what should we call it . . . spiritual experience—last?" asked Jane.

"And did it give you peace of soul?" probed Lucas.

"Yes, it did . . . but it was only the beginning. Every day I ask the Lord for forgiveness of my sins and invite Him to live in my heart and guide my decisions. Reading my Bible and praying keep our fellowship alive and my soul is fed."

"Remarkable!" exclaimed Lucas.

Jane frowned, looked at the clock and turned on the radio. News time again.

Meanwhile, my parents in America were very concerned about my safety in London, and also my brother Tom. He was with the Tenth American Air Force and had been transferred from Africa to Ceylon (now Sri Lanka).

During these critical days in England, Winston Churchill inspired his people with these words, "We'll never give up, never, never, never!"

The British people were hanging tough, but were being tested to the breaking point.

One day melted into the next. Then one Sunday in March of 1944, I invited the Ashleys to attend church with Miriam and me. Surprisingly, they said they would.

As the tempo of the war increased, I noticed more and more people began to see their deep need of spiritual help for strength to go on living.

That Sunday in church, it was a moving experience to hear the large congregation rise to its feet and sing with the mighty pipe organ—

"0 God, our help in ages past,
Our hope for years to come.
Our shelter from the stormy blast,
And our eternal home." (Isaac Watts)

After the service, we walked home slowly and quietly. The message on "The Prodigal Son" kept revolving in our thoughts. The Ashleys seemed both concerned and puzzled.

I prayed silently that they would soon find peace with God through the atonement of Jesus Christ. His death on the cross was our only bridge back to a holy God.

Chapter 12

The Great Invasion

At the Robinson Building one important job was for SHAEF to provide a handbook for the military to use when going through France. It listed all towns, locating by code the schools and buildings where the troops might pass when in need of shelter. It was called "Invade Mecum." This job and others made me aware that D-Day was not far away.

I liked working with Captain Gene Staley. The hours were often long and tedious, but awards were given out, too.

Miriam got her promotion to corporal before me. But in time I climbed to the rank of Sergeant Tech-3rd Class. My greatest surprise came later when I was awarded the Bronze Star medal "for unselfish devotion to duty above and beyond that expected over long periods of time, collecting, assembling, and recording correspondence flowing to and throughout G-2 Division, Supreme Headquarters, Allied Expeditionary Forces."

Later, though, I was put in charge of maps. And another British Sergeant, Allen Hawley, and I were keeping the military maps prior to the D-Day invasion. It was their highest way of showing their trust and confidence in us.

In a cement cubicle on the fifth floor of the Peter Robinson Building, we had at our command the exact maps of the Normandy Beachhead, which were compiled and revised day by day as the time for the invasion drew near. When no more maps came in, we sensed that D-Day had come.

Then on Tuesday, June 6, 1944, the entire world learned of the big invasion at Normandy. Many GIs lost their lives there, but it was the beginning of the final march to Berlin.

The following evening after work, Miriam said to me, "Isn't Major Ellen Davis a remarkable person?" (She was the Commander of the Allied Women's Corps.)

"Yes," I agreed. "She's a fair-minded person and commands the respect of us WACs as well as the British WAAFs."

"I probably shouldn't say this," added Miriam, "but once in a while it bothers me to see the English gals eat our rations and use our American facilities, but this togetherness no doubt will help win the war."

"It's a team effort," I answered. "By the way, did you hear what General Eisenhower said just before D-Day?"

"No, guess I missed that," replied Miriam.

"Well," I continued, "he said, 'The American Women's Army Corps has built for itself an impressive record of conduct and of service, and has given to the womanhood of America every right to be proud of their accomplishments.'"

"Nice to hear that," said Miriam as she smiled at me. All this helped confirm our thoughts that we had done the right thing by joining the WACs.

A week after the great invasion, I put on my slicker and boots and hurried to work. My desk was piled high with work to be done.

Just at that moment, Sergeant Anderson, one of Eisenhower's aides, came in and sat on the edge of my desk.

"Man, it's about time!" he exclaimed.

"What is?" I asked.

"The Krauts are getting a dose of their own medicine. By night the British bombers and by day the American bombers are really giving it to the German cities. They used to gloat over their bombing of old England, but find out now it's no fun when their own cities are being blasted to pieces."

"Honestly," I added, "will this death and destruction ever end?"

"Sure wish I knew," he answered. "I really miss my wife and kids back in good old Wyoming. Not a day goes by that I don't wish myself back there!"

"Know what you mean. I often have pangs of homesickness myself," I said.

"Incidentally, did you hear the big news?" he asked.

"No, what?"

"Have you met Veronica Long—Colonel Clark's new secretary?"

"Not really—just saw her from a distance yesterday."

"Well . . . last weekend, she up and married Sergeant Maynard. She only met him six weeks ago."

"You don't say."

"Yeah . . . she's probably acting on the current philosophy of grabbing a bit of happiness while you can. Tomorrow you may be dead."

"There are some people who seem to feel that way these days," I replied.

"But there's more to it. Two days after their wedding, Maynard was sent to the front lines in France."

"That' s too bad."

"Anyway . . . let's all hope he survives and they have a good marriage—like mine," added Anderson.

Then the Sergeant waved at me and headed for his own office.

Looking at all the work on my desk, I suddenly felt overwhelmed. How could Veronica keep her mind on her job? And here I was—having the same problem right now.

By early afternoon, I grew restless with apprehension. Around 1600 hours the sirens warned us of another air raid. We ran to the nearest bomb shelter.

Near the entrance Sergeant Anderson caught up to me and asked, "How long do you think this one will last?"

"They all seem like an eternity to me," I replied, gasping for breath.

We scarcely got into the shelter before the ground all around us shook in convulsions. The noise was deafening. I closed my eyes and put my hands over my ears.

"That was close!" exclaimed Anderson. "Must be some new kind of bomb . . . not like the ones they've used in the past."

"This is much worse than those California earthquakes," I added, trying to keep calm. "Did I ever tell you about the time my Dad became unglued when a quake hit while we were driving out there? Actually, the concrete highway just ahead of us crumbled and fell into the Pacific. And that was our first and last trip to the state of California."

"Holy cow! Sure glad we don't have those awful things in peaceful old Wyoming."

"What would happen to this shelter if we got a direct hit?" I asked rather apprehensively.

"We wouldn't live to tell about it," he answered.

The next falling bomb shook the shelter so much that dirt and pieces of timber fell down on us.

"If this keeps on much longer, we'll all be killed or injured," I moaned.

"But we're still better off in here than out in the streets," he added.

"What would happen if they hit the Robinson Building?" I queried.

"Awful thought . . . don't even talk about that. So many important papers are stored there," he replied.

"Hope those planes soon hurry up and go home," I added.

"We should be so lucky!"

Suddenly another bomb exploded above us and a large timber from the ceiling fell to the floor. Two men were hit by it and began to scream in pain.

"Is there a doctor in here?" shouted Anderson.

"I'm a nurse," volunteered a middle-aged woman.

The place was rather dark, so Anderson said to her, "Come this way. A couple of men got hurt by that falling beam."

The nurse followed Sergeant Anderson over to the injured men. "Let me have a look at them," she said.

She then loosened the tie and shirt collar on one who appeared to be about 50 years old. The other man had a light sweater on and by now both were unconscious.

After checking them over, the nurse said to Anderson, "We must get them to a hospital as soon as possible. When the 'all clear' signal sounds, go to the nearest phone and call for an ambulance. I'll stay with them until it comes."

"Sure thing," answered Anderson.

The next five minutes seemed like half a day to the rest of us in the shelter. A couple of donated jackets were put on the injured men to keep them warm. I really prayed that they would survive.

Suddenly two more bombs exploded near us. I dared not even think of what a direct hit would do!

Finally, all was quiet. And the "all clear" signal sounded out. Sergeant Anderson galloped up the steps to the nearest phone, while the others went back to their jobs. I stayed with the nurse as she checked the men's pulses. We then carefully wiped some blood from their head wounds.

After the ambulance came and took them to the hospital, I walked back to the Robinson Building. Thankfully, it had not been hit. But I found it difficult to concentrate when I remembered those two injured men. And no doubt there were hundreds of others in London either hurt or killed during that intense raid.

I worked for another hour, then covered my typewriter and started to walk toward the Ashley home.

Outside there were new heaps of rubble and several fires burning only a short distance from where I was going. One of those bombs must have landed close to the Ashley home.

Suddenly, I saw Jane running toward me, out of breath and looking very pale.

"It's Lucas!" she shouted. "He's been hurt—badly!"

"Why . . . what happened?" I asked.

"While he was hurrying home from the grocery store, a couple of falling bricks hit him on the head. Must have come from a building nearby that was hit by a bomb. The hospital just called and told me to come right over."

"Where did they take him?" I asked, trying to be calm about the bad news.

"To Mercy Hospital. Let's go over there at once!"

Now the war came even closer. Someone we cared about had been seriously injured. Would Lucas live? Was he ready if death should come?

With great difficulty we picked our way through the littered streets. Wires were down in many places, with dangerous sparks sizzling from some of them. Walls and roofs of buildings had been blown away.

"What a mess!" I exclaimed. "Broken glass, boards and smashed bricks strewn all over." Uprooted trees also blocked most of the streets.

"Once these were beautiful avenues," wept Jane. "Now they look terrible!"

Plodding on slowly, we finally came to the huge front doors of Mercy Hospital.

"A fitting name for a hospital, isn't it?" I said, as I read the large sign above the entrance — M E R C Y H 0 S P I T A L.

Jane nodded as she wiped more tears from her eyes. After we came into the lobby, a pretty red-haired nurse in a white starched uniform greeted us kindly.

"May I help you?" she inquired.

"Yes," replied Jane. "Please tell us where Lucas Ashley is—he's my husband."

The nurse checked the record book, then said, "He's on fourth floor, Room 425. But remember—only a short visit. We aren't sure yet how serious his wounds are."

After taking the elevator to fourth floor, the two of us quickly walked toward Room 425.

After quietly entering it, Jane whispered to me, "Doesn't he look pale and thin? But at least he's alive."

Lucas slowly opened his tired eyes—even gave us a little smile.

"It's so good to see you both," he whispered weakly. "But how did you get here so soon with all the debris and fires out there?"

"Wasn't easy, my dear," replied Jane as tears filled her eyes.

"We walked," I added. "With so many trees down and rubble all over, no cab could ever have made it through."

"By Jove," said Lucas, "do you know that even my ambulance couldn't get all the way to the hospital?"

"What do you mean?" asked his wife.

"The last two blocks I was carried on a stretcher by the driver and his aide."

Jane looked at me in amazement.

"How are you feeling now?" I asked Lucas.

"Pretty woozy, but glad to be alive."

Although he had always been a very kind man, Lucas had never thought much about God or the hereafter.

However, I did overhear a conversation between Jane and him about a week before this accident.

Lucas said then, "I've been observing Ruth carefully ever since she came to our house. And her lifestyle impresses me."

"What do you mean by that?" asked Jane.

"Well . . . I don't know just how to say it, but . . . she seems to get inner strength and courage from some place."

"I've noticed that, too," added Jane.

"It's amazing that she didn't get bitter toward life after losing her husband. And they had been married only two years," he said.

"True," replied Jane.

"And then she enlisted in the Women's Army Corps and came to London to work, when it would have been much safer for her to have stayed at home."

"I never thought of that," said Jane.

Lucas continued, "And in spite of all the immorality that has come with the war conditions, she manages to keep her high ideals."

"A rare person . . . I must admit," added Jane.

* * * * * *

Meanwhile, in the hospital after visiting a few more minutes with Lucas, Jane said, "We must leave now, Dear. You'll need lots of rest so you can get well soon."

"We'll come and see you often," I added as I gently pinched his big toe through the sheet.

After leaving the hospital with its heavy medicinal odor, we stumbled along the rubble-filled streets. In the darkness we smelled the pungent smoke coming from several nearby fires.

In the eerie shadows of the black night we trudged on, block after block. The distant hoot of an owl only made us walk faster.

"Good thing there's a little moonlight tonight or we'd never find our way home," I said.

"Yes, but when the clouds cover the moon, it gets so dark, I feel like we're in a cave. These old blackouts in London make night walking almost impossible," she added.

"But they're necessary—otherwise the bright lights would make good targets for the enemy night bombers," I answered.

When we finally dragged ourselves through the side door, we considered getting some dinner ready. However, by now our appetites were about gone, so we only had a sandwich and some tea.

Silence hung over the house like a dense fog. That night even the crackling wood in the fireplace failed to cheer us. The black clouds of war had personally invaded our London home.

In Mercy Hospital now, Lucas reviewed his past life of materialism. Somehow, it hadn't really satisfied him—deep down inside. And while lying flat on his back in a hospital bed, he had time to think . . . about many things.

Where would I be now if those bricks had killed me? he mused.

The loud ticking of the clock in his room became more and more annoying. He tossed restlessly on the narrow white bed. Because he could not sleep, he longed for the light of morning. But what then?

Chapter 13

A Request

I didn't sleep well that night, either. I heard the hallway clock chime out . . . one . . . two . . . three.

Finally at 0600, I got up and dressed for work. Had a light breakfast by myself, so as not to disturb Jane and Miriam. I knew Jane must be simply exhausted from the whole ordeal.

At the office I had extra reports to do, but sure found it difficult to concentrate. Lucas was in the hospital. How badly was he hurt? Would he even make it?

While typing some "rush" reports, I saw Sergeant Anderson come bouncing into my room.

"Know somethin'?" he asked.

"No, what?"

"Yesterday, June 13, 1944, was a black-letter day for the Allies."

"Meaning?"

"There were over 1500 casualties in this city as a result of the German V-1 missiles. What do you think of that?"

"Not surprised. Remember how frightening it was in the bomb shelter yesterday?" I added.

"How could I forget?" he replied.

"By the way," I continued, "did you know that Mr. Ashley was one of the injured?"

"You're kidding!"

"Only wish I were."

"What happened?" he asked.

"Coming home from the grocery store, he was hit in the head by some falling bricks and is now in Mercy Hospital."

The Sergeant whistled softly as he frowned, "Man alive, that's terrible. How's Mrs. Ashley taking it?"

"Quite well, I think. But she surely was shaken at first," I replied.

"Have you seen him yet?" he asked.

"Yes, we both went to the hospital last night."

But just at that moment in walked John Arnold.

"What are you two looking so glum about?" John asked.

"Lucas Ashley was badly injured yesterday during the missile attack and is now in the hospital," I explained.

"Sorry to hear that. Is he going to be all right?" queried John.

"We hope so, but head wounds are often unpredictable," I replied.

Finally, Sergeant Anderson stretched out his long arms and pulled himself up from the sturdy chair.

"Back to the 'salt mines,'" he yawned as he headed out the door.

After he was gone, John retorted with a frown, "Thought he'd never leave. Been wanting to ask if you'd have dinner with me this evening. Suppose Mrs. Ashley will be at the hospital most of the time now, anyway."

"Probably so. At any rate, I'd love to go out to dinner with you," I smiled.

"Good! I'll be there at 1900 hours."

Teasingly, John pulled a strand of my long hair and strolled out into the corridor.

With the stack of work before me, I secretly hoped for no more interruptions—at least for the rest of this day. Some papers were marked "rush" and they meant just that!

The afternoon seemed to fly by. Then at 1730, I covered my typewriter and left the building. I walked the few blocks to the Ashley home in record time. After entering through the front door, I went by the dining room and noticed a note on the table. Jane wrote that she'd be at Mercy Hospital with Lucas.

After running up the stairs, I took a warm bath which seemed to wash away some of my tiredness.

I looked in the closet and decided to wear my favorite light blue organdy dress. It was fun to have a special occasion to use a civilian dress.

While sitting in front of the mirror, I combed my hair into the new upsweep hairdo that was now popular for evening wear. Lots of curls on top of my head.

When John knocked at the door, I slipped into my white sling pump shoes and then let him in.

John raised his eyebrows as he looked me over, but said simply, "Hi!"

Did I detect approval in his twinkling brown eyes?

In case the weather cooled off later on, I took along a white knitted shawl.

Before we climbed into the Chevy coupe which he had borrowed from the car pool, John turned to me and said, "Cinderella herself—I do believe! Who would have thought that the kid with pigtails from next door would change into a beautiful young princess? Will wonders never cease?"

This compliment made me feel good down inside. They had been rare since Steve died.

John had some difficulty trying to dodge the big holes in the streets, but a half hour later we arrived at a quaint little restaurant on London's south side. It was a quiet neighborhood, away from the noise of downtown London.

A waitress with dark, curly hair, heavy make-up and a short skirt took our order for two chicken dinners.

Halfway through the meal, John said, "This food isn't bad, considering all the rationing. And does taste a lot better than what we have had in France."

"I thought the salad was yummy," I added.

"By the way," asked John, "do you hear much from your folks?"

"Well, yes and no. Meaning . . . I don't hear a thing for weeks and then suddenly I get a bunch of letters all at one time. Probably because of censoring and other mail delays."

"Well . . . censoring is a real safety measure. Can't afford to have important information get into the wrong hands, you know," he added.

"Anyhow—Dad says they are fine. But between the lines, I get the feeling they are pretty concerned about Tom and me."

"Mine, too. My brother Duane is in the Navy in the South Pacific. Dad wonders if the two of us will ever make it safely back home again."

"Some won't, of course. But at least the war news is better now than it was a couple of years back," I added.

"Hey, let's talk about something more upbeat. Like—how's Duchess handling things with Lucas in the hospital?"

Just the thought of dear old Duchess inspires me. So I said, "She's a darling, but really misses Lucas. Meets me at the door when I come home from work. Wants a walk and wags her tail so hard you'd think it would fall off."

"Dogs sure are great pets," added John. "I really loved the Black Lab we had when I was in grade school—my best friend, actually."

"It's hard to turn her down when she brings the leash to me, so I usually walk her every evening after dinner."

John then looked at his watch and said, "It's getting late. Perhaps we should get back . . . before Mrs. Ashley sends the police out after you."

He grinned while his eyes twinkled with amusement.

After coming into the Ashley driveway, I turned to John and said, "This has been such a lovely evening. Still can't believe that you and I should both be working in London right now."

"Life often takes some strange turns. Glad this one proved to be so delightful!"

I took a deep breath and then courageously asked him, "How come a handsome guy like you never married?"

"Wait a minute, Kitten. There's still plenty of time. Some of us are 'late bloomers,' you know."

"Meaning?"

"Oh, I did some dating in college, but with both school and work it left very little time for romance. And now with this war on, I'll probably wait till it's over before getting serious with anyone."

I just smiled at him, hoping I hadn't probed too far.

Soon his thoughts seemed to drift elsewhere. He must have had some rough experiences in France recently. And perhaps he wished he'd never volunteered for those secret missions.

At that moment, however, I saw the light go on in Jane's bedroom, so I turned to John and said, "Thanks again for a marvelous evening. Better hurry in now."

John opened the car door and escorted me to the house. He held my hand tightly, but said nothing. Then quickly walked back to the waiting Chevy.

That night, I had difficulty trying to put him out of my thoughts, but did manage a few hours of sleep toward morning.

One day faded into the next. Fortunately, Lucas continued to improve in the hospital. His injuries proved to be less serious than they were believed to be at first.

On a little calendar hanging by his bedside, Lucas had crossed off each day he had been there. Only five more and then he could go home. His doctor had promised!

At breakfast on the day of his dismissal, I said to Jane, "I'm quite sure I can borrow a car from the car pool this afternoon. Meet me at my office at five and we'll go and pick up Lucas."

"Too bad our own car is laid up for the duration," said Jane, "or we could have used it."

"What happened?" I asked.

"Shortly before you came here, it broke down. And because of the war shortages, they can't get the needed parts to repair the thing. Hopefully, after the war is over we can buy a new one."

"That's okay. The car pool people are very kind—especially when it's for a good cause," I added.

"I'm so grateful that you can help us out now. Won't it be wonderful to have Lucas home once again?"

"I'll say. Can you imagine how excited Duchess will be? See you at five," I added.

Later that afternoon I had just driven up to the curb of the Robinson Building in a blue Plymouth when Jane came across the street. Right on time.

After she got in we drove to Mercy Hospital. Leaving the car, we walked in and took the elevator to fourth floor.

In his room we found a restless Lucas. He couldn't wait to get home. But because of hospital rules, the nurse insisted on him sitting in a wheel chair while she then pushed him over to our car parked outside.

When the three of us were settled in, Lucas retorted, "Could have walked out here by myself. Those stupid rules, anyhow!"

"Now, now," soothed Jane as she gently patted his arm. "You might be weaker than you think. And if you fell . . . well, that'd mean more days back in the hospital."

"By Jove, perhaps you're right," admitted Lucas somewhat meekly.

I drove on slowly and carefully. It was a real challenge trying to avoid the bumps and potholes in the streets.

At last when we entered the driveway, Lucas exclaimed, "Oh, you beautiful home! I'm so glad to get out of that hospital and hope I never have to leave home again."

During the ensuing days there, Lucas seemed to gain strength more rapidly.

One evening as the four of us sipped on a second cup of tea, Lucas asked me, "Do you have any good books I might borrow? I'm getting bored just sitting around and a good book might be just what I need."

Miriam looked over at me.

"Sure do," I replied. "I'll run up and get you a couple right now." On my desk I found a copy of Doctor Hallesby's *Under His Wings* and also *The Robe* by Lloyd C. Douglas.

"You're so kind," he said as he took them from me.

After a half hour more of visiting, Miriam and I returned to our rooms. We both had had a tough day and were exhausted.

During the following weeks there was more bombing by the Luftwaffe. But the English underground subways had proved to be very effective air raid shelters from the enemy planes and saved many lives.

After the newscast one night, Jane asked, "How much longer do you think we can hang on without surrendering? Mr. Churchill's speeches have done wonders to keep us going . . . but there is a limit to what people can endure!"

I did not answer, but thought to myself, *These English folk must be the most tenacious and resilient people I have ever met. In a short time Poland, Belgium, Holland, Norway, Denmark and France all fell before the Nazi blitzkrieg like a row of dominoes. But the British have hung in there . . . week after week, year after year!*

The Royal Air Force had proved to be both amazing and effective. As early as September of 1940, Mr. Churchill spoke to the House of Commons, honoring the R.A.F. by stating, "Never before in the field of human conflict was so much owed by so many to so few."

This tribute continued to be reality year after year for the R.A.F. However, at the moment Lucas felt more optimistic than his wife. He said, "In spite of the costly invasion, I believe the Allies will soon overpower the German war machine."

Then looking at Miriam and me, he added, "Sure glad you Yanks came over to help us."

"Suppose you're right," sighed Jane who was emotionally drained from her many trips to the hospital to see Lucas. "We'd better press on to the finish now. Say, wouldn't it be wonderful if the war both in Europe and in the Pacific would be over at this time next year?"

"Some of our Top Brass seem to think that is possible," replied Miriam.

"By the way, have any of you heard those awful rumors about what is going on in the German concentration camps? They say thousands of people are being exterminated in large gas furnaces every day," said Jane.

"My word," retorted Lucas, "the vast tragedy of this conflict is going beyond human comprehension. If there is a God, why doesn't He do something about it?"

"And why haven't the German people risen up against Hitler?" asked Jane. "Where are the pastors and church members?"

"There are some pastors, like Dietrich Bonhoeffer, who are speaking out against the evils of the Third Reich," I replied.

"And it'll probably cost him his head!" exclaimed a distraught Lucas.

"Perhaps," I said, "but I still believe God is in control of the world. Sin has caused all this death and destruction. And sin always brings on judgment. But God will soon give us a day of deliverance, I'm sure."

"What do you mean?" asked Lucas.

"Often when things go well for people, they don't see any need for God in their lives," I added.

"Perhaps," answered Jane.

"But then during times of severe trial, people come to the end of themselves and cry to God for help . . . and salvation," I continued.

"Hmm . . . guess you're right," replied Lucas. "If I hadn't been in the hospital, I may never have started seeking for some answers in my own life. I really did some serious thinking on that hard old hospital bed."

"For instance," I said, "someone from the Underground recently reported that a Dutch lady by the name of Corrie ten Boom brought a Bible with her into a concentration camp."

"How'd she do that?" asked Jane.

"Don't know the details, but the guard didn't see it. Anyway, she, who is a Christian believer, began reading this Bible to the other women prisoners there and many of them accepted Jesus Christ as their own personal Savior."

"What does that mean?" asked Lucas.

"It means acknowledging that I am a sinner, deserving of hell, but because Jesus died on the cross for all my sins, I can be saved by accepting His atonement for sin. Then God forgives me for Jesus' sake. But in order to grow in grace each day, I continue to read my Bible, pray and ask Jesus to control my life."

"Your God seems to work in mysterious ways," added Lucas.

"Somehow, our Lord can use the worst of circumstances and bring much good from them," said Miriam.

"No doubt when a person faces death it often changes his way of thinking and his values," replied Lucas.

"Until we have made our peace with God by accepting the finished work of Jesus on the cross, we aren't ready to die. And we haven't really learned how to live, either!" I added.

The Ashleys looked at both Miriam and me—rather puzzled and amazed. But at least they seemed open to search for the truth.

Chapter 14

Beyond Our Strength

During the fall of 1944, the victories and defeats in Europe, Russia, and the Pacific varied from day to day. Fortunately, the Allies were now gaining more ground as each month passed.

In December the Battle of the Bulge began in Europe, and the Germans fought fiercely.

One evening as Lucas, Jane, Miriam and I sat by the fireplace, I asked, "With all the heavy bombing of German cities, do you suppose they'll soon surrender?"

Lucas answered, "I've heard rumors that some Nazi officers would like to surrender now before more lives are lost in a hopeless cause. But old Hitler insists that every soldier continue fighting until the last German is dead."

"How awful!" exclaimed Jane. "He must be mad! The sensible thing would be for him to surrender before thousands of soldiers and civilians are slaughtered in a no-win situation."

"This World War II has really turned the earth upside down," said Miriam. "And . . . to think we believed that growing up during the Great Depression was pretty tough!"

"Oh, let's change the subject," replied Jane. "By the way, yesterday I went shopping for a new dress to cheer myself up. But the selection was pitiful."

"What do you mean?" I asked.

"The styles were dull and the material worse. No doubt the best cloth is being made into military uniforms," she answered.

"Could be," added Lucas.

"But," continued Jane, "while I was looking around in Eaton's Store, a capital idea struck me."

"What was that?" asked Miriam.

"About two years ago, I bought some fine navy blue gabardine material. It has been tucked away in my dresser ever since. But now I'm going to get a pattern and sew myself a new suit for spring. I can wear so many different blouses with a good basic suit."

"Smashing idea, my dear!" exclaimed Lucas as he put down his newspaper. "You can be creative and save money, too. And it's patriotic to be thrifty, you know.

"Sounds terrific," I answered. "May I watch you make it?"

"Of course."

"I have sewed some simple dresses for myself in the past, but never tried making a suit. Padded shoulders are popular now, too, aren't they?" I added.

"Let's all of us work on this project. Then it ought to turn out beautifully," said Lucas with a sparkle in his eyes.

"By the way, Ruth, how are your parents doing these days?" asked Jane.

"Quite well . . . I think. Because help is scarce, Mother volunteered to work as a nurse's aide in our local hospital for three days a week—and she loves it!"

"What about your father?" asked Lucas.

"He had retired a few years ago, but now has a part-time job working in a grocery store," I added.

"What business was he in before he retired?" asked Lucas.

"He owned and operated a drugstore in Fairmont. After being there for 30 years, he's sort of glad to have this new job to keep busy."

After a few minutes of silence, Lucas turned to me and asked, "Incidentally, those books you loaned me were tops. Now I'm wondering—do you have a Bible I can borrow?"

"Sure do. I'll go upstairs and get one right away."

I got up from the sofa and went up to my room. After picking up my Bible, I came down and handed it to Lucas.

He was yawning, so I added, "It's getting late. Tomorrow will be a busy day, so I'm going to retire now. See you at breakfast in the morning."

Later on, as Lucas and Jane were in their bedroom, he said to her, "Honestly, I don't know where this world is heading. War . . . hatred . . . killings. Life is so confusing. Guess I need to find some answers—and soon!"

Meanwhile in my room, I read from Doctor Hallesby's devotional book and prayed that as Lucas read the Bible the Holy Spirit might awaken him to see his need of a Savior. Only in Jesus Christ do we have the answer to peace with God.

The following day at work while I was typing some reports, Sergeant Anderson came in to chat.

"Hi, Ruth," he said. "Say, those old Germans are really putting up a stiff fight right now, aren't they? But anyhow, I sure hope this is the last Christmas we'll have to spend in foggy old London town. Wouldn't it be jolly if we could all be home for Christmas of 1945?"

"I'll vote for that," I agreed and made a V for victory sign with my two fingers.

"You know—this crazy war sure has had some weird angles," he added.

"For instance?"

"Remember back in June of 1940 . . . when we read about the miraculous escape of the British Army at Dunkirk?"

"Yes, guess I do recall hearing about it."

"Imagine the English people rounding up all those boats of all sorts and sending them to the French coast, where they picked up the thousands of seemingly doomed British soldiers?"

"Unbelievable!" I added.

"But it did happen. And this ragtag fleet brought most of them safely across the Channel. Still can't believe they actually pulled that one off."

"Won't that daring escape add some excitement to the history books for years to come?" I answered.

"Something else puzzles me."

"And what is that?" I asked.

"Remember when Russia thought she had made an agreement with Germany? Then the old Krauts turned around and attacked the Reds on the Eastern front."

"To be honest," I said, "I still have trouble accepting the fact that Russia is on our side. Their ideology is so different from ours . . . yet, we're now both fighting the Nazis."

"Ya, ya, who'd ever have thunk that could happen," added Anderson as he shrugged his shoulders. "But I don't trust that communistic outfit, either. Some of us were saying just the other day that we'll probably be fighting Russia herself before this mess is over with."

"What a mixed up world! This may sound strange, but once in a while I wish I had been born in the 1800s when life must have been simpler."

"You can't win there, either," he added. "'Twas no bed of roses during the Civil War—with brother fighting against brother."

"You're right. Guess I'd forgotten about that one," I sighed.

"At any rate," continued Anderson, "I thought I had found the good life—ranching in peaceful old Wyoming. And it was great! Until the lousy Japs bombed Pearl Harbor and the draft board called up my number."

Taking a deep breath, I added, "My college days were rather carefree, but life surely has taken some strange turns since then. It's probably best we can't foretell the future."

"Hey, now, just to lighten this heavy conversation, I just gotta tell ya what Corporal Hanson said yesterday."

"You mean Jim Hanson?"

"None other—anyhow, he said, 'If I ever get out of this war alive, I'm going home, find me a nice girl to marry and have so many kids that they'll never draft me again! Perhaps the government will even pay me to stay out of the Army!'"

I couldn't help laughing at this unique strategy. "Supposing he actually had 14 kids," I said, "perhaps the government would find it cheaper to classify him as 4-F rather than pay out a huge amount of money for child support."

Sergeant Anderson smiled and then walked over to the small window overlooking the busy street below. He asked, "Say, what do you think of Eisenhower?"

"Well, my respect for him keeps increasing. He surely has some awesome responsibilities and decisions to make — remembering D-Day, especially," I added.

"Wouldn't care to have his job for anything! Must be tough for him to see those long casualty lists every day."

"Know something?" I replied. "Once when I was in his office I noticed an open Bible on his desk."

"Ya did?"

"Yes, and he told me he often reads it to find inner strength and courage for the hard decisions he has to make. He had recently been reading about the strategy and surprise attacks used by the Israelites in the Old Testament wars."

Shrugging his broad shoulders in amazement, Anderson just said, "Well, I'll be . . ."

Chapter 15

Transformed

After entering the Ashley home that evening, I found a letter on the hall table from my brother Tom.

He wrote to me quite often, but because of mail censorship I never really knew what he had experienced on the hot, sandy African battleground.

Over a year ago in one of his letters from Africa, he had written: "Some of our supply ships were sunk by the Nazi U-boats in the Atlantic. So for a whole week, all we had to eat was some old potato peelings. Sure hope some good food gets here soon—you know my big old appetite!"

However, after the Allies won the African campaign, Tom was transferred to the American Air Base on the island of Ceylon (Sri Lanka).

From there he had written: "Although I'm assigned to work in the meteorology department on our base, I recently volunteered to go on a bombing mission as a gunner on one of the B-29s. And would you believe it . . . that day only four planes from our squadron made it safely back home. Ours was one! I picked up some shrapnel in my back as a souvenir, though, but guess I can live with that. What I find really tough to handle is facing the fact that many of my close buddies never return from these missions. I get a sick stomach when I look over and see their empty bunks as night rolls around."

But now . . . this letter which came today from Tom had some interesting news. He had met a pretty dark-haired girl from Cambridge, England. She was in the WRNS (Women's Royal Naval Service) which was also stationed on Ceylon. They had been having several fun dates together.

Would this romance develop into marriage? I wondered. If it did, none of his or her family would be at the wedding.

At any rate, I eagerly looked forward to every letter from Tom, Sue and my parents. Mail was the one way of family communication during the long, weary war years.

On Sunday evening, December 3, the Ashleys, Miriam and I huddled closely around the glowing, crackling fireplace. The rain began to beat sharply against the window and a few flashes of jagged lightning preceded the loud, rumbling thunder. Impressive sound effects.

"Oh, it's so good to be inside a warm house on a wild night like this!" exclaimed Miriam as she gazed out of the large window. "But I keep thinking of the many GIs crouched down in their cold, muddy foxholes. Kinda feel a little guilty."

Lucas put down the newspaper he was reading and said, "We can't fret about that. Besides . . . right here in London we could be blown to smithereens at any moment—from a direct hit!"

"Sorry . . . you're right. We should be thankful for this fine evening we are enjoying right now," added Miriam.

The four of us were silent for quite a while. The glow from the burning logs warmed the elegantly furnished living room.

Suddenly Lucas pulled his chair closer to us on the sofa.

"Ladies," he went on, "I've been doing a lot of searching the last few weeks. Never thought much about God before. But a terrible feeling of emptiness has gripped me during these war years. How can I find peace for my restless soul, Ruth?"

I was a bit surprised at his question, but replied, "The Bible says, 'All have sinned and come short of the glory of God.'"

"Yes . . . I fully realize that I'm a big sinner and have lived only for myself and material things."

"But there's hope," I added. "Jesus died on the cross for sinners, just like you and me."

"Sure glad to hear that," he replied.

"The Bible also says that anyone who comes to Jesus will not be turned away."

"Do you think that includes me?" he asked sincerely.

"I know it does. And Matthew 11:28 says, 'Come unto me all ye that labor and are heavy laden and I will give you rest.'"

"Yes, yes . . . that's what I need . . . rest for my soul."

"Then open your heart right now and ask Jesus to come in and take charge of your life," I added.

"Can I do that here?"

"Of course. And we'll pray that the Holy Spirit will give you assurance of salvation from some special Scripture passage. Here—I'll show you some verses from the Gospel of John that might be helpful to begin with."

"It sure would be great to live without fear of death and let the Lord run my life instead of me," said Lucas.

"Jesus will lift your burden of sin and give you real joy and purpose for living each day," I added. "Then let's also read from I John 5:13 . . . 'These things have I written unto you that believe on the name of the Son of God; that ye may know that ye have eternal life, and that ye may believe on the name of the Son of God.'"

"That must be the answer to the puzzle of life," replied Lucas. "Eternal life is given to those who personally accept the finished work of Jesus Christ on the cross as payment for their sins."

"Yes, it really is simple," I added. "But we cannot grasp it until the Holy Spirit convinces us that we are lost sinners. Then we will seek refuge in the wounds of Jesus. That's how I found peace with God."

"And that's what I need now—the forgiveness of all my sins and His peace," said Lucas.

"Shall we pray?" I asked him.

Lucas nodded his head.

After my prayer, he began a simple prayer of repentance, asking Jesus to forgive his many sins and inviting the Lord to come into his heart.

I believe he made a sincere commitment to Jesus and relinquished his own independence, for this brought a new peace and joy into his face.

At the same time, Jane looked quite confused about the situation and not knowing what else to do, she turned on the radio for the BBC news.

The reporter said that the war was going better for the Americans in the Pacific area. A number of islands formerly occupied by the Japanese had now been recaptured. And General MacArthur had kept his promise and returned to the Philippines.

The next day after work, I stopped by Cathy Ranier's office on second floor and we went out for dinner together. She was one of the secretaries whom I had recently met.

While we were enjoying a second cup of coffee after our meal, I asked her, "Have you had any good letters lately?"

"A few," she replied. "And you?"

"My brother Tom has had some narrow escapes, but I'm so thankful he's still alive."

"Some days I get no mail, but then comes a bunch of letters from my husband Paul. I just read them over and over again. It helps keep me going after these hectic days around here."

"By the way," I asked, "do you and Paul have any special plans after the war is over?"

"Just being together again will be wonderful! But . . . once in awhile I dream about owning a nice split-level home in one of the suburbs of San Francisco."

"Sounds lovely," I added.

"But before that, I'm looking forward to being on a plane together—looking at the beautiful Golden Gate Bridge as we glide into the airport."

"Guess the song writer said it best when he wrote . . . "I Can Dream, Can't I?" I said softly.

Chapter 16

A Shattered Dream

As the fierce fighting on various battle fronts increased, so did the work load at the Intelligence Department. At the same time, the French Underground people were busy blowing up railroads, bridges and ammunition dumps. All this hindered the transportation of Nazi supply trains, trucks and troops. And Ultra continued to relay reams of material to the American Headquarters.

One brisk morning, December 18, while a penetrating gale blew off the English Channel, Sergeant Anderson hurried into the Robinson Building. His coat was buttoned up tightly.

He stopped on fifth floor to visit me.

"Would you like to hear a real cutie today?" he asked with a gleam in his eyes.

"Guess I can handle that," I replied.

"Well . . . one of our officers, Major Thompson, said he learned about a Frenchman who gathers information about the location of Nazi bunkers and writes it down on a scrap of paper. He then attaches the piece of paper to the leg of a homing pigeon (which has been parachuted to him by an Allied plane). From the nearby woods he then releases the pigeon, which flies on home with the information to England."

"Smart bird, I'd say!" I exclaimed. "And to think that even the birds are getting involved in World War II."

"Anything for the cause, dearie, anything," drawled the Sergeant as he yawned, stretched his long arms and finally went back to his own office.

At this time also, many summit conferences with Allied generals were being held at unusual hours—like 0400! Crucial information must not fall into enemy hands. What did it all mean?

After one rather grueling day at work, I dragged my weary feet home and picked up the mail which lay on the hall table.

There was a letter from my brother Tom. I could hardly wait to read it.

He wrote: "Four of us GIs had a weekend pass which we spent in Calcutta, India. What a city! People dying on the streets, and poverty and disease beyond belief. Yet we did find some interesting places to visit. Bought a few souvenirs which I'll bring home to you and the folks . . . sometime.

"Will never forget the little children with haunting dark eyes begging us for food. We gave them some candy bars which we happened to have in our pockets.

"These years in the Army have been a real education for me . . . Something I'd never get in any college. Not the least is my deeper appreciation of the good old U.S.A.!

"By the way, we also managed a trip to see the famous Taj Mahal. Wow! What a work of art and beauty. Hope you have a chance to see it some day, too."

After reading his letter over again, I thought how drastically the war had changed our lives—and millions of others. People saw conditions and countries they probably never would have otherwise.

As the battles raged on, Christmas of 1944 came on the scene. Miriam and I got only half of the day off and had to work all of New Year's Day to keep up with the reports.

The Battle of the Bulge continued to take many American lives. Tears filled our eyes when we saw the long casualty lists.

But time moved on. January 19, 1945, was a bitterly cold day. At noon I walked down to second floor to have lunch with Cathy. Surprisingly, her door was open. Then I saw her sobbing with her head on her desk.

I hesitated for a moment, but walked in slowly and asked, "What's the matter?"

Cathy looked up at me with tearful eyes and handed me a yellow telegram. "Just read this," she said.

I could not believe my eyes when I read: "The War Department regrets to inform you of the death of your husband Captain Paul A. Ranier on January 8, 1945. His plane was shot down during a bombing mission over Hamburg, Germany."

How terrible! I put my arms around her. Then I remembered afresh Steve's tragic death in Brazil.

I wanted to tell her about him, but was too overcome with emotion to talk. We just clung to each other.

Cathy wanted to lock herself in a room alone and try to think through this nightmare. There had to be a mistake, she reasoned. Paul might have parachuted to safety and would come back one of these days. How could she go on without him? Life had suddenly turned into a deep, dark tunnel . . . with only thick blackness at its end.

"I'll ask for the rest of the day off," I added, "and we'll both go to the Ashleys."

"Might as well," sobbed Cathy. "I can't concentrate now, anyway."

We both received permission to leave.

As we walked out of the building into the busy street, she asked me, "Death is never easy to deal with, is it?"

"No, it isn't," I agreed.

"And it's even worse when it's someone very close to you. And Paul was so young . . . only 26, you know."

We walked on in silence.

When we reached the Ashley place, we told Lucas and Jane the sad news. They wept with us.

That evening Jane prepared a tasty dinner, but we ate little. The grief seemed overwhelming.

Later when the table was cleared, the five of us sat around the warm fireplace, sipping on a second cup of tea.

Finally I said to Cathy softly, "My dear, I know what you're going through."

Cathy looked at me in surprise, then shook her head. "How could you know how I feel?"

"I never told you this before, but I lost my dear husband from malaria in Brazil. We'd been married only two years."

"Is that really true?" she asked.

"It is. And when he died, I was left all alone for a week on the edge of a jungle with only a village of primitive natives nearby."

"How awful!" she exclaimed.

"At the time, the heartache and loss seemed more than I could bear."

With a look of amazement she added, "You . . . you never told me about this before—why?"

"No . . . the time never seemed right—until now."

"I can't believe what you're telling me is true!" she added.

"The reason I didn't say anything about it before is because we have all seen so much tragedy around us the past few years. So I tried to remember and talk about more pleasant things."

"How did you handle all that?" asked Cathy.

"Well, at first I thought my heart would actually break in pieces, but then I cried to the Lord for help. His promises in the Bible sustained me . . . often for only one hour at a time."

"But I feel almost numb. Like having a nightmare that won't end."

"Would it help to talk about Paul? Sometimes it's good to talk and work our way through grief," said Jane.

"Maybe you're right," replied Cathy. "Let's see. I met Paul when I worked as a secretary for Senator Sloan in Washington, D.C. At that time I shared an apartment with another girl, Dianne—she was Paul's sister."

"So that's how you two met," added Lucas.

"Right. One colorful autumn weekend Paul took both of us to the Army-Navy football game. And that was some game! Even remember the score. Navy won 21 to 20. Afterward we went to a charming little cafe for dinner. But I hardly knew what we ate or talked about. Paul was special and I was smitten."

"That's the way I felt about Steve, too," I replied.

"Well . . . Paul and I dated steady from then on and were married on June 10, 1941. He was everything I had hoped for in a husband."

Again Cathy began sobbing and couldn't say any more.

"Losing one's mate must be one of the hardest trials in life," said Jane tearfully.

We were all silent for a while. Finally, Cathy cleared her throat and continued. "But then the blow came. Pearl Harbor! After that, Paul enlisted in the Air Force. And I joined the Women's Army Corps, hoping to be stationed near Paul. And we did manage to spend a couple of wonderful furloughs together."

"Precious memories, I'm sure," replied Miriam.

"Know something else?" continued Cathy. "On our wedding day, we made plans to celebrate our 25th anniversary in Hawaii. But now he's . . . he's gone—forever!"

While she cried as if her heart would break, I reached over and stroked her soft dark hair.

"Is there anything we can do to help?" I asked, even though feeling quite helpless. "Somehow, we must go on living whether we feel like it or not."

"But how can I?" she cried.

"Ask the Lord for help and comfort. He is always available. Also, your friends here will support you. Besides—your job of being involved in the war effort will help heal the hurting inside," I added.

"Suppose I'm lucky to have such demanding work. It'll keep me from brooding too much," she replied.

"When I got home to my parents and then taught at Lincoln High, I found kids who had real problems in their own lives," I said.

Cathy looked up at me—puzzled.

"Many teenagers were hurting, too, in different ways. And as I listened and encouraged them—yes, loved them—I found the pain easing in my own heart."

"What else helped?" asked Cathy.

"Well . . . after reading my Bible, I began each day by writing down all the things I had to be thankful for. This helped me concentrate on the positive instead of the negative side of life."

"Suppose you're right. But at the moment, I feel like I'm drowning in a pool of despondency."

Miriam and I walked Cathy home that evening. But the next two nights, Cathy insisted on being alone in her own apartment. She wanted to write to Paul's parents and her own. And this would be most difficult as there would never be another Paul! How could she face another day—or a whole year—without him?

But deep in her heart, Cathy knew Paul would want her to stay on her job . . . until the awful war was over. Paul was loyal and dependable and he had found these same qualities in his wife.

The second evening of her widowhood she lay on her feather bed and wept bitterly. *Has any other war caused so much grief and destruction as World War II is doing?* she thought to herself.

Chapter 17

Allied Victory

To our surprise, the following day we received marching orders. Miriam and I hurried back to the Ashleys for a short "goodbye," grabbed our meager belongings and stuffed them into our duffel bags.

We left London at noon and were hauled away in crowded trucks. When we came to the English Channel, a ship took us to France.

At Versailles, we were housed in cold barracks with only a wood stove to keep us warm. We even resorted to cutting up wooden chairs and whatever else we could find to keep somewhat warm. As water was scarce, we bathed in our helmets!

At night I often dreamed about a warm bedroom and the luxury of a good bath. But life was hard here in France. I did have an edge on some of the others, however, having spent those years in primitive Brazil, near the jungle.

The bitter cold days of winter passed by, but oh so slowly! When the warmth of April finally came, it was most welcome, to be sure.

In Versailles our office was a store building that the Allies had taken over temporarily. Rugged conditions.

April 12 began as a normal day. No one foresaw what would happen that very afternoon.

However, as we were getting ready for bed about 2200 hours that evening, Major Ellen Davis called us all to attention for a special announcement.

With deep emotion she told us, "I am sorry to report that President Franklin Delano Roosevelt died this afternoon in Warm Springs, Georgia, of a massive cerebral hemorrhage."

I looked at Miriam. We were all speechless, then broke into tears. "What a terrible thing for our country!" exclaimed Miriam.

"Still can't believe it's actually true," I replied.

"Will our new President, Mr. Truman, be able to handle such a big job? Mr. Roosevelt had had so many years of experience both at home and with foreign policy," added Miriam.

"One thing's for sure—those are mighty big shoes to step into," I replied.

"I wonder what General Eisenhower and General Patton think about this terrible news—at such a critical time?" asked Major Davis.

"At least we can be thankful that the Allies are getting close to Berlin," said Miriam.

"Don't see how Germany can hold out much longer," added Major Davis. "But it's too bad that President Roosevelt didn't live long enough to celebrate the final day of victory—which should come soon."

And on that very day many Nazi battalions had surrendered to the Allies, in spite of Hitler's insane orders for them to fight until the last man was killed.

Days of uncertainty and surprise came and went—slowly.

In our dreary barracks on the evening of April 30, Miriam had her portable radio on. The British newscaster was so excited we could hardly follow what he was saying. He blurted out:

"Tonight is a turning point in history! Just two days ago we heard the startling news that Mussolini and his mistress were executed in Italy. And today we learned that American soldiers stormed Der Feuhrer's bunker in Berlin. But all they found was the charred remains of Herr Hitler and Eva Braun. Rumors from the bunker said that these two were married only yesterday and then both committed suicide. Hours before this, Hitler had commanded one of his aides to soak their dead bodies with gasoline and burn them. He could not face the possibility of capture and torture. So ends the life of a twisted genius who brought so much misery to the whole world!"

All of us WACs listening to the radio looked at each other in shock and disbelief. Could this incredible report be true? Would it at last mean an end to the long years of fighting, suffering and death?

In the following days the Allied Armies moved forward from one victory to another. For a change, we now looked forward to hearing the nightly newscasts.

One sad incident, however, was that of the execution of Pastor Dietrich Bonhoeffer only three weeks before the war in Europe ended. He was 37 years old and engaged to be married. One of the few Germans who had had courage enough to speak out against the evils of the Third Reich—and it cost him his life! Just as Lucas Ashley had predicted.

Marching orders came again for us. This time the crowded trucks took us to Rheims and that is where history was made.

We WACs were housed in the famous "Ecole Primaire Superior," in the very building where the Nazi generals surrendered.

On May 7, 1945 at 2:41 a.m., the defeated German officers arrived. The military personnel—GIs as well as WACs—stood at attention, waiting for the final settlement. We could see the table where the generals sat, but we did not see their faces.

Suddenly, General Eisenhower appeared on the steps and with a broad grin he waved and said, "Now you can all go to bed!"

But who could sleep after that exciting news? What a night of rejoicing it was!

Cease fire orders went out to all the Allied troops. And in the little French village of Rheims, General Eisenhower declared a day of worship and thanksgiving which we all attended. There, too, stood our leader in the French cathedral with bowed head, giving glory to God for the victory won.

Marching orders again! From Rheims we were sent to Frankfort, Germany. Here we were housed in apartment buildings once occupied by German families. They looked at us with hateful eyes amidst the awful desolation brought on by the air raid bombings.

I felt like reminding them, "Who started it all, anyway?" But that was now past history.

Headquarters was now located in the IRB-Farban Building and the great task of demobilization began.

The summer months kept us busy with loads of paper work.

Meanwhile, the tension kept building up in the Pacific. Then on August 6, the mysterious atomic bomb was dropped on Hiroshima by a lone American B-29 Superfortress. The pilot was Col. Paul Tibbets, Jr.

Three days later another atomic bomb fell on Nagasaki. Because of the extensive death and devastation from these mushroom-like cloud bombs, the Emperor of Japan reluctantly agreed to sign the surrender treaty—before more of his cities were annihilated. The historic signing took place on the *U.S.S. Missouri* on September 2.

That night Miriam hugged me and exclaimed, "It's finally over! Now I hope we can go home."

We remained together and returned to the United States on the *Queen Mary* which sailed from Southampton, England, on September 5.

From New York, I took a plane going to Camp Beade near Sacramento, California, for my discharge papers. However, while flying over my homeland, I viewed the gold and purple sunset in the western sky, And it reminded me of the verse of Scripture the Lord had comforted me with as I flew from the Amazon region in 1941. His promise had proved sufficient from that day until now. "But those who hope in the Lord shall renew their strength. They will soar on wings like eagles" (Isaiah 40:31).

Chapter 18

Home Again

The much prayed for peace now reigned on earth during the autumn of 1945. Even the birds sensed it when they headed south in their V formations. Fleecy white clouds of freedom floated freely in turquoise skies. A new beginning!

Although I had been in the Army for only two and a half years, it had seemed like forever. So many changes, heartaches and adjustments during those war years.

They had been difficult for people in the States, too. There was always the nagging fear of getting a "regret telegram" from the War Department, plus the real possibility of being invaded by the enemy. Overtime work, restrictions, loved ones in service and rationing filled their days.

The bus ride across the various states was tedious as I longed to see my family again and get caught up on some sleep. Because of the rugged living conditions in France, I had lost over ten pounds.

However, September is always a beautiful month. And I drank in the beauty of the countryside as we rode along the ribboned highways. The leaves were just turning to red and gold. Each new scene became more fantastic than the one we had just passed. I especially loved to see the cattle and horses grazing in lush pastures, plus an occasional grove of maple, oak and birch trees. What a contrast to the bombed out cities in Europe.

When we finally pulled into Fairmont, Mom and Dad had been waiting at the depot for an hour.

As I stepped off the crowded bus I heard Dad exclaim, "There's Ruth. A little older and thinner, but still pretty as a picture."

Running toward them I cried, "It's so good to be home!" And I could hold back the tears no longer.

I wanted to hug them forever.

But finally Dad let go of me and added, "Ladies, we can't stay here all night. I'm starved even if no one else is."

"Me, too," I replied. "A good cup of coffee would really hit the spot."

"It's after six o'clock now," said Mother, "so let's go out and eat at some nice restaurant. We haven't done that for ages."

After getting into Dad's old 1937 Ford, we drove to a cozy place called Jensen's Fine Foods.

As we pulled into the parking lot, Dad said, "I don't know how they do it, but this place has the best food in town."

He then found a spacious booth. We ordered steaks, baked potatoes, broccoli in cheese sauce, fruit salad and chocolate cream pie for dessert.

Having lost about ten pounds, I felt I could eat without counting the calories! And everything was especially tasty with Mother and Dad sitting across the table from me.

"My, it's been a long time since I've eaten such a tender steak," remarked Dad.

"Yes," added Mother, "during the war years, rationing made meat and other things very scarce, but we got along anyway."

"Our victory garden was a big help. Most everyone went into gardening on their back lawn to help with the food scarcity," said Dad.

But I hardly tasted the food. There was so much to talk about. However, that broccoli was extra good.

Later on, Dad pulled out his well-worn pocket watch and said in amazement, "Do you realize it's nearly ten o'clock? The place will soon close for the night."

We then got up, paid the cashier, went outside and got into the car. Looking over its familiar interior I said, "Oh, Dad, I'm so glad you still have our old '37 Ford. When I was in London I often thought about the fun afternoons we had when you took me into the country and taught me how to drive this very car!"

"Yes, I remember that too. The stick shift and clutch gave you some problems at first," he added, chuckling.

"Guess the coming thing now is the automatic shift. Must have been invented by some woman!" I exclaimed.

"But I really do like this old car. It's always been so dependable," replied Dad.

"Wonder when they'll start making cars again?" I asked.

"Cars have been real scarce cause they quit making them early in 1942. But I hear there are some 1946 models coming out soon," said Dad.

"By the way, wasn't the success of air power during the war unbelievable?" I continued.

"Absolutely. I believe the R.A.F. and American Air Force had much to do with winning the war," added Dad.

"Recently the Germans were making some powerful rocket engines, so it's a good thing the war ended when it did," I said.

"What do you suppose has happened to those bright young Nazi scientists now?" queried Dad.

"I've heard that some of them have already come to the States to work on our space research program," I replied.

Just then we pulled into the driveway.

Mother yawned and said, "I'm really very tired, but too excited to sleep. Can hardly believe you are actually home again with us, Ruth."

"Seems too good to be true for me also," I replied as tears came into my eyes. "There were many times during the air raids when I wondered if any of us would get home alive."

"Isn't it a shame that all of these high tech discoveries couldn't be used to help the world instead of trying to blow it up?" asked Dad.

"You can say that again," I added. "And what if the atomic bomb gets into the hands of some radicals in the future?"

Dad shook his head and sighed, "Honey, if it weren't for my trust in the Lord, I'd be very frightened about the coming years."

"Me, too," I said.

"By the way, what did you think of General Eisenhower—as a person?" asked Dad. "Rumors are already flying that one of the political parties wants him to run for president."

"He was both brilliant and likeable. And if he ever does run for some office, I'll vote for him—no matter what party he's with," I added.

As we stepped out of the car I noticed something. "Say, I like that new coat of white paint on the house. And the black shutters. Neat!"

"That was a family project a year ago. Sue even spent part of her vacation helping us," said Mother.

Dad then got out and took my duffel bag from the car trunk. When I opened the kitchen door, it squeaked.

Dad smiled at me and said, "I need to get some oil on those hinges again."

As I went from room to room looking things over, I remarked, "Doesn't seem as though much has changed since I left."

"Probably not," answered Mother. "Most everything was either scarce or impossible to get during the war. But we 'made do' and bought war bonds to help out the cause."

"Couldn't even buy a radio during those years," laughed Dad. "And our old one on the kitchen counter was in the repair shop more than it was at home."

All three of us then sat on the brown plaid sofa in the living room and I asked, "Well . . . how did you dear people spend these last three years?"

"Nothing dramatic happened," replied Dad. "But we kept busy which left less time for worry about you and Tom overseas.

I had many things to tell them, too, but it would have to be done over a period of time. So many important happenings to remember.

About midnight Mother suggested, "Let's get some rest now and talk more tomorrow. It's been an exciting day and so wonderful to have you home safe with us again, Ruth!"

"Okay, Mom," I agreed. "Just can't wait to get into my old bed once more."

"My, weren't you fortunate to have lived for a time with the Ashleys?" added Dad.

"I'll say! But such a short time. It seemed we were always on the move."

"See you in the morning, Dear," said Dad as he gave me a warm hug.

The next few days floated by like a dream. There were so many exciting, sad and funny events to share. Joy, sorrow and humor—all wrapped up in those bleak war years.

After two weeks of getting re-acquainted, however, I became a little restless and went outside for a walk.

Probably out of a former habit, I found myself in front of Lincoln High. As I looked at the windows of the room that had once been mine, a tinge of nostalgia gripped my heart. Should I stop in and see the superintendent? Would he, by chance, be in his office now?

"Well . . . I'll give it a try, I thought to myself. After entering the familiar happy halls of learning, my high heels clicked sharply against the hard tiled corridor which led to his busy office.

The building had not changed at all since I taught there. But looking around, I felt it could use some fresh paint and a few repairs.

Materials had been scarce or unavailable for the duration. But the economy was shifting gears again as the great need for jobs and housing escalated with the return of millions of service men and women. And many business places, homes and schools were in real need of repair or remodeling.

As Mr. Jackson's office door happened to be open, I politely knocked on the door jamb.

He looked up and smiled and then came over to shake my hand.

"Delighted to see you again, Ruth," he said. "My, my, you must have had some terrific experiences since you left us. Your father told me about a few of them when I saw him in the grocery store."

"That's for sure. It was quite an adventure. Some days I felt I was almost drowning in work and responsibility, but the people in the Intelligence Department were good to work with."

"I don't want to seem pushy, he added, "but we could surely use a good substitute teacher here at Lincoln. When you were here before, we appreciated the personal interest you took in your students. Not many teachers have the compassion that means spending time with the kids after school hours."

"So kind of you to say that. But remember . . . they also helped me during my time of healing from the loss of Steve."

"How true. When we help others, we usually are benefitted ourselves."

Then I added, "Guess I'm getting bored with loafing at home, so your offer to be a sub is just what I need now."

"Good! I'll call you soon. You'll probably be working about two or three days a week."

At that moment the phone rang and Mr. Jackson picked up the receiver. Knowing he was very busy, I excused myself and left.

After walking through the hallway, I opened the heavy glass front door. Breathing in the crisp fall air, I felt real good inside. Work is such a blessing!

After dinner that evening, my father exclaimed, "My dear, that substitute teaching job sounds wonderful! You'll have something definite to do . . . and yet have time for shopping and a much needed rest. Let's not kid ourselves—those years in Europe were tough ones.

"You're probably right, Dad. And now I can hardly wait for Christmas! I missed you dear people always, but especially at Christmastime. England was often rainy and foggy around the holidays and I was lonesome with no family near me."

"We missed you and Tom also, but at least Sue got home for both Christmas and New Year's," added Mother.

"You'll never know how much I wished for snow on the ground and the city streets all lit up with colored lights. And Christmas Eve services in our church! But now I'm home again . . . with all those extras!"

Chapter 19

A White Christmas

I had more substitute work than expected, so October and November passed by rather quickly. But each day was different and challenging—up to my ears!

When December 17 arrived, Mother and I planned a special shopping trip together. It was also the first day of school vacation.

The fall months had been unusually mild for New York and the ground was brown with dead grass and leaves.

However, the very morning we walked downtown, a light snow began to fall.

"Isn't it beautiful?" I asked Mother. "Now everything looks so clean and sparkling."

"True, but I'll wager that by March we'll all be tired of shoveling out the sidewalks and driveway!" laughed Mother.

When we reached Marshall's Department Store, she motioned for me to stop. "Ruth, just look at that window display."

After enjoying the scene for a time, I replied, "Aren't those little elves skating on the ice pond adorable? How do they make it all look so real?"

"Must take many hours of hard work to come up with something as intricate as this," she answered.

As we walked on, another window caught our attention.

"How beautiful," I said softly as we gazed at the Nativity scene.

"Why, I believe those are real live lambs in that stable! And the life-size figures of Mary, Joseph and the Baby Jesus seem almost human," added Mother.

"So impressive . . . and this is truly what Christmas is all about. God sent His only Son into the world to atone for our sins and make it possible for us to inherit eternal life," I said.

Mother looked at me and smiled in agreement.

A few minutes later we walked inside the spacious store. What elaborate decorations! Green holly wreaths trimmed with red velvet bows. Silver tinsel clinging to evergreen trees. Red and white striped candy canes suspended from the ceiling. Next came the sound of Bing Crosby's recording of "I'm Dreaming of a White Christmas."

I looked at Mother and said, "Doesn't that song give you goose bumps? Last year Sergeant Anderson sang it at our Headquarters party in London. A nostalgic time. We all wondered if we'd ever again see a real white Christmas in a free world. And now that wish has come true!"

For several weeks I had been thinking about gifts for my dear family. They would have to be very special . . . this Christmas.

To keep the element of surprise, Mother and I went our separate ways to shop.

After an hour of searching and comparing values, I found a handsome gold pocket watch. Would Dad like it? Actually, his old one now seemed beyond repair. I couldn't resist. After the clerk put it in a fancy box, I paid her and put it in my shopping bag.

Later on at the jewelry counter, a lovely string of pearls caught my eye. They somehow reminded me of the song, "String of Pearls" by Glenn Miller. To be sure, Mother was a pearl of great value in my life. And in a dark purple velvet box their beauty was enhanced.

At noon we met in the coffee shop for lunch. By then our shopping bags were already getting full of presents.

As we talked over sandwiches and coffee, I said, "Mom, do you remember all the 'fun' shopping trips we had together when I was a teenager? You were not only my dear mother, but also a real friend during those difficult years."

With tears in her eyes, Mother smiled. She also remembered.

About the middle of the afternoon, I checked my gift list again. The names of Tom and Pat were there—they had been married in Ceylon after the Germans surrendered. However, because they would not be discharged from service until this coming June, I needed to buy their presents at once and have them airmailed to Ceylon in the morning, I really should have sent them out in November because overseas mail is slow going.

Fortunately, Sue would be with us for Christmas. Because we had been apart for so many years, her gift must also be something special.

As we kept on shopping, the time flew by. And soon both of us were weary.

When darkness descended on the little city, the street lights came on. Brilliant and colorful! How I had missed all this in Europe.

Soon a large white moon replaced the golden sunshine in the sky. While walking home, we felt the shopping bags become heavier by the minute.

At the kitchen door Mother moaned, "Honestly, I'm so tired I couldn't go one more step."

We entered the house, sat down on the sofa and kicked off our shoes.

"Having spent those years in Europe with blackouts and other restrictions, I can't get enough of the colored lights and decorated stores around town," I said.

"But why does this wonderful season always pass by so quickly?" asked Mother.

"Don't know why, but it sure does! And oh, how I love the pleasing pine scent from the Christmas tree that Dad put up in the living room. It feels wonderful just to be alive!" I added.

"Sometimes I think of the many Christmas gatherings we took for granted when you children were all home. But the war really changed everything," replied Mother.

"It changed many people, too," I added.

"There will be many sad homes with vacant chairs around tables this Christmas," she added softly.

"Yes, and think of the thousands of soldiers who now lie in foreign graves. Freedom is so costly!" I said.

"It's a miracle Tom has come through it all alive—and you also. But you both had some close calls!" exclaimed Mother.

"Changing the subject—but I'm really looking forward to our Christmas candlelight service at church," I said.

"Didn't you go to any like that in London?"

"I wasn't able to find one. Of course, London had so many restrictions after 1939."

Suddenly, I added, "The other day I read about two missionaries who experienced a very joyful Christmas—even though they were put in a wretched prison camp."

"What do you mean?" asked Mother.

"Well, both were in cold, dismal cells, but they could see each other. Then one of them got an idea. He broke off pieces of straw and formed the word 'Emmanuel.' And as the two missionaries looked intently at this word—meaning 'God with us,' their hearts were filled with joy unspeakable. Later on, they were set free, but never forgot this blessed Christmas experience."

Mother looked at me and smiled, "Yes, that is the true meaning of Christmas."

"The prisoners had no distractions or trappings while in those empty cells, but the Lord was with them and radiated His love into their hearts," I added.

"What a touching true story," said Mother. "And we must not let 'things' crowd out the real truth of the Word becoming flesh and dwelling among us poor sinners this year, either."

When Christmas Eve finally arrived, the four of us sat around the decorated tree with its all-blue lights on. After Dad read the account of the Birth of Jesus from Luke 2, each of us offered a short prayer. Then we gave out our gifts of love to each other. I wished the evening would never end. Home again with my dear family!

But soon the clock in the hallway reminded us it was 10:30, so we put on our heavy coats and boots and hurried to church.

In the chancel area, poinsettia plants were arranged on a wire planter in the form of a cross. Two pine trees decorated with golden bells stood on either side of the cross. The lights were turned off and each person in the audience held a small lighted candle, while the purple-robed choir sang softly "0 Holy Night."

Joy flooded my soul as the candles glowed in the darkness. The sermon was inspiring and this was indeed a holy night!

At midnight after the impressive service, we walked slowly home in the cold December moonlight. No one spoke for it was a precious sacred moment.

The next morning being Christmas Day, our grandparents, aunts, uncles and cousins all poured into our home for a festive dinner.

For the first time since the war ended, I had an opportunity to talk with two of my cousins who had also been in service. Lloyd had been with the Navy in the South Pacific, while Arthur had been in the Infantry in Italy and France. Another cousin, Robert, had lost his life during the costly invasion at Omaha Beach in Normandy.

The harsh war years forced us to grow up in a hurry. Arthur showed it the most physically, with his dark hair now graying around the temples.

We tried to minimize the war talk and speak more about the future. We all hoped for many happy, peaceful years ahead.

How wonderful to be together once more on that Christmas of 1945! For several years, we had been scattered all over the globe. But that day . . . our dream of a white Christmas *at home* came to pass.

Chapter 20

The Reunion

Although I wasn't quite ready for it, New Year's Eve suddenly arrived. Having had a rather hectic week with relatives coming and going almost every day, we decided to spend a quiet evening at home.

However, while Dad, Mother, Sue and I sat around the fireplace, we heard a sharp knock at the front door.

"Now who can *that* be?" asked Sue, looking very puzzled.

"Have no idea," I replied, "but I'll slip into my shoes and soon find out."

After opening the front door, I stared in amazement. There was John Arnold. His brown eyes twinkled and he was neatly dressed in a gray pin-stripe suit.

"Is it really you?" I asked.

"None other. Sort of lost track of you the past year. Often wondered if you had gone home after the war ended or were off to some faraway land in search of a new adventure," he teased.

"No way! I could hardly wait to get back to dear old Fairmont. And then Mr. Jackson offered me a substitute teaching job, which I really love."

John smiled and then sat down in our rust-colored rocker. After visiting with us for about an hour, he said, "Ruth, how about going out for a New Year's Eve drive?"

"I'd like that," I answered and went to the hall closet to get my new maroon winter coat.

John escorted me to his 1940 Dodge, which he had bought before joining the Army. During the war his parents had stored it in their double garage.

"It's wonderful to see you again," I said, as we backed out of the driveway. "Often wondered what happened to you after we WACs were sent to France."

"To be honest," he added, "on my last trip to the front lines I was shot in the leg by a sniper, which put me in a military hospital for over a month. But it's hard to keep a good man down, you know! However, it did delay my discharge until just before Christmas."

"Sorry to hear about your injury."

"No big deal. It healed slowly, but nicely."

We drove down the familiar streets of our childhood. Already some new homes were being built to meet the pressing need for housing.

As we looked at the homes and other buildings, he added, "Hasn't changed much around here, has it?"

"No, and I'm glad about that! Fairmont never looked so good to me as it did this past September when I came back," I replied.

John drove toward the airport, located at the south edge of town on a high bluff. From there we could see the hundreds of lights below. Several small planes also landed or took off while we watched them.

"Honestly, those rugged years in the Army now seem like a bad dream," he said. "Sometimes I'd like to blot them out of my memory and get on with a normal life."

"It's best not to dwell on sad things, but those of us who experienced the horrors of war firsthand will never be able to forget it completely," I added.

"What did you think about those atomic bombs that were dropped on Japan last August? The Top Brass sure kept that a deep, dark secret, didn't they?" he added.

"And no doubt Japan would never have surrendered otherwise," I replied. "What do you suppose will happen when other nations develop atomic bombs?" he continued.

"Let's not even talk about it. One of the generals in France said he didn't see how this old world would hang together beyond 1952," I said.

John was quiet for a time, so I asked, "By the way, what are your plans for the future?"

"Rather think I'll be going to Washington, D.C. An old Army buddy of mine said that there are some good job openings in government now. Gonna check that out first of all."

"Really? Well, I sure wish you every success," I replied.

"By the way, Ruth, did I ever tell you how much those dinners together in London meant to me? Must admit, though, it took me quite a while to realize you had grown up—and were no longer the kid in pigtails from next door."

I couldn't help laughing, but said, "And I was overjoyed to see you . . . somebody from my own hometown."

"Sure glad you made it back safely. Actually, we were both often in much danger," he added.

"For sure. Oh, say, when do you plan to leave for the Capital?"

"Day after tomorrow."

"That soon?"

"Yup—got to get going with life, Dearie. I'm already past 30!"

"Well . . . I hope you like living in D.C. By the way, would you write to me once in a while?" I asked.

"Of course. But what time is it getting to be?" he queried.

"Ten to 12," I replied, looking at my wrist watch.

"Let's hop on over to Jack's Cafe and see the New Year in over there," he said.

"Good idea . . . but we'd better hurry."

John drove swiftly downtown. Two green lights favored us, too.

At Jack's, we found a secluded booth and ordered two trout dinners.

After eating, I said, "Didn't feel all that hungry when we came here, but this food was super! Haven't we got much to be thankful for this New Year's Day of 1946? And may the coming years be ones of peace and freedom."

"Shalom, my dear. We only have a couple of cokes, but let's drink to that wish," he added.

After a long pause, John said, "Somehow I can't help wondering why I was lucky enough to return home after the war, when so many of my buddies are now lying in foreign cemeteries?"

"Hmm . . . I believe the Lord has a special plan for each person's life," I said softly.

"Maybe some day I'll begin searching for mine, but not just yet. There are lots of things I'd like to do first," he replied.

During the next five minutes, John was so deep in his own thoughts that I felt almost alone in the cafe.

Suddenly, glancing at the clock above the cashier, he added, "Perhaps we'd better be getting back to our families."

After helping me put on my coat, we walked together to his car. Just before getting in, I exclaimed, "Oh, look! It's beginning to snow again. See how the bright lights shining on the newly fallen snowflakes make them look like a blanket of sparkling diamonds. Beautiful beyond words!"

Chapter 21

A New Family Member

On January 15, John Arnold began working at a government position in Washington, D.C. And before long he was caught up in the social whirl of politicians.

Three weeks later at an elite cocktail party, he met a lovely brunette with pretty violet eyes. Her name was Mary Olsen and her father was the Ambassador to Sweden. During her high school years, Mary had lived in Sweden with her parents. But now she was a staff nurse at Metropolitan Hospital in Washington.

Before the party ended, John maneuvered his way toward the pretty nurse and began talking with her.

After some light conversation, he impulsively asked, "Mary, would you like to have dinner with me next Friday evening?"

Mary was both surprised and flattered, so she paused a minute, while gazing into his twinkling brown eyes. Then she said, "Why, yes . . . I think that evening is open. When should I be ready?"

"I'll be at your apartment at eight. What was that address again?"

"It's 7200 Marlboro Avenue, Apartment 602."

"Terrific. See you then."

A half hour later as John walked toward his car, he felt pleased with himself for being able to make a date with this lovely lady named Mary. And he had met her for the first time just that evening!

Life sometimes takes an unexpected but good turn, he thought. And friendship with Mary might be important to his future. Her father must know many famous people, to be sure. In D.C., it was often more important *whom* you knew, instead of *what* you knew.

Before getting into his car, John looked at it with admiration. A brand new 1946 Chrysler—maroon with a cream-colored top. Having been on a waiting list for only three weeks, he felt very lucky to own this dream boat. At present, new cars were almost impossible to buy and the demand was simply overwhelming. Unless you had a close friend or relative in the car business, you stood little chance of getting one of the new models coming off the assembly lines daily.

He loved the feel of the interior as he ran his fingers gently over the new maroon velvet upholstery. After starting it, he cruised slowly back to his own apartment, enjoying every block of the short trip home.

During the weekdays, John worked in a tall, imposing office building on Pennsylvania Avenue. The frantic pace of his business responsibilities made the week slip by rather quickly. And before long, Friday evening had come.

He wore his new navy blue suit with a red and silver striped tie. After hurrying out of his apartment, he jumped into the classy Chrysler. He drove some distance before locating Mary's apartment building. The first thing he noticed there was the very attractive landscaping. Soon he entered through the large glass doors and walked on a thick blue carpet to the elevator which took him to sixth floor. Then he walked down the short corridor to Room 602.

After ringing the doorbell, Mary asked him into her living room. She almost took his breath away—dressed in a purple velvet tunic dress with a wide silver metallic belt.

John felt like whistling, but restrained himself. Instead, he helped Mary put on her soft mink stole. And before long they were outside the building walking toward his new car.

After getting in, Mary said, "My, I never expected to be riding in such grand style. How ever did you manage to buy a new car so soon after the war ended?"

"Had my name on a waiting list for a while before the dealer called me. Of course . . . it did help that the manager of Leland Motors happened to be Captain LeBeau whom I knew from overseas. At any rate, I sure am fortunate to be the owner of this little baby!"

Mary just smiled as they sped on toward Club 21. Gazing through the car window, she noticed the bare and lifeless-looking trees.

"I can hardly wait for spring to come," she sighed. "The pink cherry blossoms, regal red tulips and yellow daffodils always bring new life into our winter-weary lives."

John nodded in agreement.

After parking the car, they entered the exclusive club. The freshly starched white tablecloths were decorated with red linen napkins. And each table also had its own red rose in a white glass vase.

"I'm impressed!" exclaimed Mary as she looked at John. "Our hospital food is quite good, but in a setting like this everything should taste simply terrific."

"Glad the lady is so pleased," added John with a trace of modesty. But he thought to himself, *Today is Valentine's Day which probably accounts for the red and white decor in the dining room. How fortunate that my first date with Mary came on this romantic holiday. Some days it does pay to get out of bed!*

After a little discussion about the bleak weather, Mary asked, "John, where did you serve in the big war? I vaguely remember you saying that you had been stationed in Europe."

"That's right. After being shipped overseas, I was placed in the Army Intelligence Department in London. Later I volunteered for some secret missions in France, trying to get inside information on enemy strategy and weapons. Plenty exciting . . . but very risky also! However, enough of this talk about me. Where were you those years?"

"Oh . . . guess my life was more sheltered. During high school I lived with my folks in Sweden. By the way, wasn't it unbelievable that both Sweden and Switzerland managed to remain neutral during the whole conflict?"

"You can say that again," replied John. "Can't see how they did it—especially when Norway, France and the others were taken over by the Nazis."

"Well then, after graduating from high school I returned to the States for a year of college, plus three years of nurses' training here in D.C. After getting my R.N., I became a staff nurse at Metropolitan. And that's about it."

"Good for you!" exclaimed John.

"However . . ." she continued, "had the war kept on much longer, I seriously considered enlisting for overseas duty in the South Pacific."

"Any special reason?" he queried.

"Yes, several doctors whom I knew from our staff here were commissioned as officers and served aboard Navy ships. I recall one of them writing that he had operated for 72 hours straight without any sleep after a terrible battle with the Japs on Leyte Gulf."

John paused for a moment. "Wonder why the press didn't give much coverage to the doctors and nurses who saved so many lives on various battlefronts?"

"Guess there'll always be the unselfish ones who work behind the scenes, carrying on with little or no recognition during their lifetimes," she answered.

"For sure."

"This is changing the subject," added Mary, "but what do you think of the Lincoln Memorial? Those historic messages carved in marble are so impressive. Just imagine the heavy responsibilities Mr. Lincoln must have carried during the Civil War!"

"Probably more than any other president. On the other hand, Franklin Roosevelt had plenty during this last war also. Might have helped shorten his life," said John.

At that moment a courteous waiter took their orders and soon John and Mary were enjoying delicious prime rib dinners.

John thought to himself, *Mary's delightful company makes the food taste even better!*

Afterward while they drove down Pennsylvania Avenue, John glanced into Mary's lovely violet eyes. He momentarily forgot where he was going, but a near collision with a black Chevy coupe jarred him back to reality. From then on he watched the traffic more closely.

"One of these Saturdays we should drive up to see Mount Vernon," suggested John. "President Washington's home overlooking the Potomac is something else. But . . . suppose you've been there before."

"I have, but I never tire of seeing these interesting places. They really make history come alive!" replied Mary.

While glancing at her watch, she could hardly believe it was already midnight.

"Better be getting back," Mary added. "I'm scheduled to work in surgery tomorrow and need to be wide awake then."

John reluctantly drove Mary to her apartment building. But he refused to escort her to her room until she had promised to have another date with him the next Friday night. She agreed.

February passed by rather quickly for John with a busy work schedule and many social activities. Spring arrived in March with nature awakening from its winter dormancy. He wrote to me once in a while but soon stopped completely. I wondered what had happened, but didn't write to him either.

For some months I didn't even know about Mary. Naturally, she had the edge—living there in D.C. and being available for dinners, concerts and ball games.

John was impressed with her father, an ambassador. Power, position and connections—all these appealed to his ego.

One Wednesday evening while John was relaxing in his own apartment, he found some old pictures in his desk drawer. They had been taken in London and I was in several of them.

Looking at these, he thought to himself, *Ruth is quite a girl, too. Not shallow as some he had met. But for an unknown reason there seems to be an invisible wall between us . . . both puzzling and annoying.*

However, at this moment Mary had come into his life! She was one fascinating gal. Loved her nursing career, but enjoyed dating, too. Life was getting complex . . . what should he do?

Meanwhile back in Fairmont, I signed a teaching contract at Lincoln High for the school term of 1946 and 1947.

One especially lovely day in May, Mom, Dad and I sat on our spacious front porch. The fragrance from the lilac bushes seemed to permeate the air around us.

I looked at them and asked, "Isn't it wonderful to have life back to normal again?"

"Almost too good to be true," replied Dad.

"Those years I spent in England and France were full of excitement, but the work stress and air raids were really tough at times," I said.

"So good to have you safe at home now," added Mother. "And it's wonderful that you are getting some extra rest also."

"Sure missed you and Tom during the war," said Dad. "And to think Tom and Pat haven't even been discharged yet. But hold on . . . I do have some great news."

"What's that?" I asked.

"They are both returning to the States next month!"

"Wonderful! I can hardly wait," I exclaimed. "Can you believe it . . . we haven't even met his wife yet. Think she'll like us . . . and America?"

"Hope so," replied Dad. "Hey, what about planning a Fourth of July reunion right here in our own back yard? I'll call Sue and see if she can come, too."

* * * * * *

Tom and Patricia arrived safely at our home on Independence Day of 1946.

The night before they came, I said to my parents, "Isn't this unusual? Here we are celebrating our independence from dear old England tomorrow and Tom is bringing his British bride along to celebrate with us." (She had been born in Cambridge, England.)

Dad chuckled as he added, "Yes, life often throws us a few interesting curves."

I could hardly wait until the next morning when Tom and Pat came into our driveway. Then I saw him open the car door for her.

She was slim, dressed in a soft green dress which accented her hazel eyes. Her black hair was combed back and up at the sides with lots of curls on top. From the back, loose waves of hair fell casually to her shoulders.

After Tom introduced his wife to us we fell in love with her and her quaint British accent.

Later on around the picnic table, I heard her say "tomaato" instead of "tomato." And her laughter was contagious. Tom had chosen wisely.

After our dessert of apple pie and cheese, Dad asked Pat, "How do you think you'll like living here in the States?"

"Haven't been (bean) here long enough to say, but so far I'm liking what I see," she answered.

"That's good," replied Mother who felt very happy about Pat joining our family.

"One thing I do like is your central heating," she said. "In England our fireplaces give such uneven heat. However . . . there is something that really confuses me."

"What's that?" asked Tom.

"The American slang. Sometimes I can't follow you Americans."

Mother smiled and added, "It's true . . . and your King's English is so beautiful. However, in America people do use a lot of slang expressions. And each section of the country has its own culture and accent as well."

Pat answered, "There's something else different. Guess I'll have to buy some of your cookbooks. Your food preparation seems so different from ours. But I must confess . . . I spent very little time in our kitchen at home before joining the Women's Royal Naval Service."

"Don't worry," said Tom. "You'll do fine. And I'm very happy to introduce my beautiful wife to all my relatives and friends here."

"Tom," added Sue, "you made a good choice—we all love Pat!"

Having spent those years in London, I said, "I know Pat really comes from a tenacious people. Even though the Nazis bombed England for many hard years, they never gave up!"

Pat smiled at me, then looked up at the cloudless turquoise sky and said, "I just love the weather today but could do without those noisy firecrackers."

"Can't believe we are finally all together again as a family," replied Sue. "It has been so many years!"

"Are you working some place now?" Pat asked Sue.

"Yes, I am. After college I got a job as a medical secretary for Dr. Ronald Redman in Philadelphia. Just love it there."

After the picnic lunch was over, we carried the dishes into the kitchen. Then Tom spread out a couple of old blankets on the lush green lawn.

And he said, "Hey, let's not talk about the old war any more, I want to find out what's been happening here at home."

"I'll second that," added Pat.

"Ruth, do you see much change in the schools after the war?" asked Tom.

"Well . . . I believe the kids are more serious and studious now than before. Many of them have older brothers who went through terrible ordeals on the front lines," I replied.

"By the way," said Tom, "one of our generals said he thought World War II, to a large extent, was won by the 18 and 19 year old boys."

"Unbelievable . . . yet we must admit that that age group would probably be the most daring in battle," replied Sue.

"And here we are . . . back to war talk again," added Tom as he winked at his wife.

"Well, the war surely changed family life back here in the States," said Mother.

"In what way?" asked Sue.

"Women began working outside their homes in large numbers. At first it was because of the real shortage of workers. Then some liked the extra paycheck so much, they kept on even when the war ended," said Mother.

"But this also means less time for mothers to teach their children moral and spiritual values," added Father.

"Can the school teachers help these kids at all?" probed Sue.

"I'm not sure," I answered. "But whenever I see students who are having problems, I try to talk with them after classes. At least they know that someone does care about them."

Father then asked, "How do you think all the uprooting, plus the death and maiming of thousands of men will affect our country in the coming years?"

"Only the Lord knows that," I sighed. "The next few decades will no doubt be both exciting and different. Perhaps the new space program will even try to land someone on the moon!"

"That'll be the day!" exclaimed a doubting Tom.

The afternoon seemed to fly by as we visited about many topics. But that evening we went to see the colorful fireworks, shot high into the sky above shimmering Silver Lake.

We loved watching the exploding bursts of pink and silver glitter. They looked like umbrellas of sparkling stars. Others were of lime green, powder blue and gold. One pink display was accompanied by machine gun-like shots into the black velvet sky. The fitting conclusion was a lighted replica of the American flag, glittering in bright red, white and blue.

Pat looked at us in amazement and said, "I haven't seen anything as spectacular as this in peacetime before!"

The first year of freedom since Pearl Harbor deserved the finest patriotic celebration possible. And Fairmont went all-out on this July 4, 1946.

Chapter 22

The Glory of Easter

After spending a week with us, Tom and Pat drove on to Pittsburgh where he got his old job back—the one he had had before joining the Army. With Sue in Philly, Mom, Dad and I were now alone in the family home.

I spent much of August getting my clothes ready for school. Sewing new dresses and skirts and lengthening a few old ones, where possible. The hem lines had suddenly dropped to mid-calf from knee length.

Actually I was really excited about being a full-time teacher again. Perhaps my experiences in England and France would provide new resource material for my classes.

School began the first Tuesday after Labor Day. From then on, the school activities and challenges made the fall and winter months pass by very quickly.

And in a short time, the spring of 1947 had arrived. While sitting on the sofa reading a novel on Palm Sunday evening, I got a sudden inspiration. Reaching for the phone, I dialed Sue's number. She was just coming out of the shower when her phone rang sharply.

Still dripping wet, she wrapped herself in a large beach towel and muttered, "Wonder who that could be at this hour?"

"It's me . . . Ruth," I said breathlessly. "Hey, I just got an idea. How about spending the Easter weekend with me in New York City?"

"You mean it? That'd be super! Got a touch of the old spring fever anyway and would welcome a change of scenery."

"Glad you're interested. Meet me in the north coffee shop of the Great Eastern Depot on Friday evening about seven. Then on Saturday we can do a little shopping and perhaps some sight-seeing, if there's time."

"Cheers to you for a terrific idea! We really haven't had much time for girl talk either since you came back. And I've missed you so much," added Sue.

"I know . . . me, too. But, hopefully, things will be better from now on. By the way, should I make reservations for us at the Hilton for those two nights?" I asked.

"Fine. That's close to some nice stores, too," replied Sue.

"This has been such a busy school term that I'm more than ready for a trip out of town," I added.

Then just as I put the receiver down, Mother came into the room. "Just called Sue," I said. "We're planning an Easter weekend in the Big City."

"Why . . . that's great! It'll do you both lots of good." I smiled at her and agreed.

Mother headed for the stairway, but suddenly turned around and added, "Incidentally, as long as you will be there, why not visit Madison Avenue Church on Easter Sunday? One of my friends, Mrs. Young, recently mentioned that they have a fine pastor there. She has heard some of his broadcasts over the radio."

"Hmm . . . we might do that—unless Sue has other plans."

The next few days I was busy correcting papers and preparing lesson plans for the Monday after Easter. I also experimented with some creative ways of making a few favorite skirts a little longer.

At last, Friday morning came and I packed a medium-sized suitcase. In the late afternoon, Dad insisted on driving me to the train depot.

The noisy steel monster was right on time. If all went well, we would pull into New York City at 6:45 p.m.

As I waved goodbye to Dad and boarded the train, its loud whistle pierced the air. After several jolting starts, it settled down to a smooth ride. The blue plush cushioned seats felt so good and I stretched out my legs.

From the train window I saw that April's warm days had coaxed out new, lush green leaves on the trees. Most of the lawns were raked clean and many yards boasted of blooming daffodils and tulips. They were so cheerful after the long winter that the next hour went by very quickly.

Then as the daylight disappeared, the huge locomotive chugged into the railroad station.

My left leg had gone to sleep, so I rubbed it awhile before pulling my suitcase down from the shelf above me. I followed the other passengers to the nearest exit and walked down the short stairs onto the sidewalk below.

After entering the crowded depot, I elbowed my way gently toward the coffee shop. Sue was already there.

We both ordered coffee.

"Great to see you, Ruth!" she exclaimed as she leaned over and kissed me.

"I could hardly wait for Friday to come. I've been so anxious to see you again," I answered.

We took our time, sipping on the steaming-hot coffee.

Sue looked off into the distance, then said, "Hey, let's take a few minutes to browse in that gift shop."

Just outside the terminal was a small shop that specialized in stuffed animals.

"Guess I'll never outgrow my love of animals—both real and stuffed," she added.

"Aren't they adorable!" I agreed. "Especially this gray and pink elephant. Bet it would look great on your bed."

I didn't even wait for her answer, but immediately bought the stuffed elephant and gave it to her.

She then hugged it and giggled like a little girl.

We looked at other items in the store, too . . . rings, bracelets and various trinkets.

Suddenly, Sue pulled at my arm and whispered, "I think that man in the black leather jacket is staring at us."

I glanced over my shoulder and saw him also.

"I don't like his looks—makes me feel creepy," added Sue.

"Me, too."

"What should we do?" she asked rather anxiously.

"Let's try to hail a cab outside. Can't do any walking on the streets with someone like that around," I replied.

We left the store and waited for a taxi to come by. But just at that moment, the suspicious-looking man came outside and walked directly toward us!

He grinned and asked, "Need a lift, ladies?"

"No thanks," I answered. "We're expecting a cab."

"I won't charge a cent," he continued, leering at Sue.

"But we have other plans," replied Sue firmly.

Nevertheless, he kept standing there and looked at us with a smirk on his face.

We ignored him and waited. I prayed for divine protection and that a cab would soon come by.

Finally, one pulled toward the curb and we ran over to flag it down. Seeing this, the man in the black jacket walked slowly down the street.

When we were safe inside the taxi, Sue whispered to me, "Bet that guy was up to no good. Sure glad there were the two of us."

"No one can take any chances in a large city like this. Robberies and murders happen every day," I added.

After a rapid and somewhat reckless ride, the cab squealed to a sudden stop in front of the Hilton.

Sue paid the driver and we hurried up the broad concrete steps into the lobby.

I glanced behind—to see if we had been followed, but saw no one.

We then noticed and admired the thick red carpet in the lobby. And the tall windows were elegantly draped in lovely red velvet with the walls in white. An elaborate chandelier glittered from high in the ceiling. Swank all the way.

After registering at the desk, a young bellhop came and carried our luggage into the elevator. We stopped at third floor. He went ahead and opened up Room 377. After entering, I noticed the pleasing decor of beige, brown and orange colors. This would be a very cozy place for us during the next two days.

A bit weary from the train trip, we both kicked off our high heels and slipped out of our traveling suits into some comfortable lounging robes and flats. Sue's robe was pink which set off her dark curly hair. Mine was blue.

"How about having room service bring us up something to eat?" asked Sue. "I only had a snack this afternoon, so feel a bit starved right now."

"Great idea!" I agreed.

Sue called in our orders and half an hour later we enjoyed munching on ham and cheese sandwiches, fruit salad and milk. But I could hardly wait for the dessert—chocolate cake with lemon filling.

Sue finished eating before me, stretched and then asked, "Ruth, did I ever tell you about my date with Don when I was in college?"

"Can't recall," I answered, still enjoying the delicious cake.

"Well, we had a fun time together. However . . . when I came back to the dorm rather late that night, I walked quietly up the stairs to the room I shared with June."

"Then what?"

"I carefully opened the door so as not to awaken her, when suddenly I felt something wet and cold pouring down on my head. Then a small pail hit me also. June had rigged up this pail of water over the transom, so the minute I opened the door it would tip over on me."

"Bet that cooled you down in a hurry!" I giggled.

"Twasn't funny then—but it is now," she laughed. "June was awake all the time and I heard her muffled laughter from under the covers on her bed."

"By the way, did the pail hurt you?" I asked.

"No . . . just my pride. And ya know what? I was wearing a blue and red wool plaid dress. And the water shrunk it so I could never wear it again!"

We continued telling some funny or scary things that had happened while we were apart.

Later on I looked at Sue and said, "You know, somehow I can't get away from the feeling that I should go back to Brazil and finish the work Steve and I began there. But I can't see going alone!"

"Hasn't the Mission Board found anyone else to replace you?" she asked.

"Not as far as I know. Of course, the war was a big reason—many ships were sunk by the Nazis."

Just then the clock from a nearby church chimed out eleven o'clock.

"Say, let's shower and get to bed now," suggested Sue. "Tomorrow should be a great day for us."

The night hours sped by like a dream and soon the bright sunshine coming through the large window awakened us.

After putting on a couple of casual cotton dresses, we went down to the hotel restaurant for a light breakfast.

"We aren't far from Field's Department Store," I said. "They have lots of interesting things to see."

"Okay," replied Sue. "Let's begin there."

After our meal, we walked outside. How good it was to inhale the warm spring air. And only four blocks away was the large store.

"Do you suppose we should look around for new outfits for Easter?" asked Sue, as her face flushed with excitement. "Never felt much like dressing up during the drab war years . . .

besides," she added with a twinkle in her big brown eyes, "most of the eligible men were away in military service."

I smiled and added, "Well, I know one thing—our WAC uniforms were practical but not feminine. In fact, someone called our shoes 'the gruesome twosome.'"

We soon entered the store and strolled amid the racks of dresses—and more dresses. Dark ones, light ones, tailored, frilly—just overwhelming. Where to begin?

After trying on several, I discovered a pretty lavender dress with an accordion pleated skirt. My favorite color. "What do you think of this?" I asked Sue.

She looked it over carefully, then exclaimed, "I like it! Will do something for you—without being too showy."

I found a fitting room and tried it on. Felt good. "I'm going to buy this dress," I added.

"Now let's check out the suit section," said Sue. "I feel in the mood for a spring suit."

After looking at several, she decided on a pastel yellow one with a navy blue blouse. It fit as though tailor made.

The clerk took our money and put our purchases in large boxes.

Next, we took the elevator to second floor and came into the home furnishings department. A large display of attractive kitchen curtains begged for our attention.

"Wouldn't these sheer white ones with the embroidered yellow and orange flowers on them do wonders for Mom's kitchen?" I asked.

"Oh, I just know she'd love'em!" agreed Sue. "Do you know the size of the two windows?"

"Well . . . not exactly, but I think I can estimate them fairly closely."

"What say? Let's go half and half on the cost and buy 'em," added Sue.

After paying the clerk, I put the curtains in my shopping bag and we left the store. Throngs of last-minute Easter shoppers crowded the busy sidewalks, making it difficult to walk.

After another hour of window shopping, Sue said, "Hey, let's walk over to that park in the next block. My feet are killing me. Not used to pounding sidewalks, you know."

"Yours is a desk job . . . yes, I can understand. Teachers are on their feet more than secretaries, I reckon," I added.

We soon found an empty park bench and sat down. Sue smiled and said, "Hasn't this been a fun day? Hope we can get together more often in the coming weeks."

"I wouldn't have missed it for anything," I replied, giving her a gentle hug.

We put our heavy shopping bags down on the grass and enjoyed the quietness of the park. I especially liked watching the ducks swim around on the small blue lake. Peace in the midst of a noisy busy city.

The hours seemed to melt away. Finally, I said to Sue, "It's getting late. We'd better call a cab and return to the hotel."

"Good idea. My feet won't take any more today. And . . . we don't want some creep following us when it gets dark, either!"

We walked less than a block before hailing a Blue and White taxi. Had some difficult getting our bulky shopping bags in with us, but managed. And 15 minutes later, we were at our hotel.

As we entered the spacious lobby, I enjoyed the feel of the thick red carpet beneath my tired feet. And above us that chandelier glittered like myriads of diamonds. After walking a short distance, we entered the elevator which took us up to third floor.

In our cozy room, we sank into a couple of overstuffed chairs and tossed off our shoes.

After relaxing a while, I finally asked Sue, "Do you think we can get up early enough tomorrow morning to attend the sunrise services at the Madison Avenue Church?"

Sue looked surprised.

So I went on explaining, "I read their announcement in the *Times* while we sat in the park. Or . . . perhaps you have other plans?"

"Nope . . . and there's no problem in getting up early. We'll just skip breakfast and take a cab right to the church," she replied.

We took out our purchases and looked them over. However, after shopping and being in large crowds most of the day, we were rather exhausted. Sue then ordered lunch sent up from room service, had our relaxing baths and crawled into a soft bed.

The alarm was set for six o'clock as the service would begin at seven.

The night seemed to evaporate away when suddenly the shattering alarm clock jarred us from our deep sleep.

"Is it already six?" I asked, not yet fully awake.

"Can't make it," groaned Sue as she pulled the covers over her head.

"Take a quick cool shower, Honey," I answered. "That'll get you going."

She ignored me, so I continued, "Hey, remember . . . we've got new outfits to wear—and it's Easter Sunday!"

"Guess you're right," she whispered while dragging herself out of bed.

She then leaned against the wall to steady herself and drowsily stumbled toward the bathroom.

After putting on our new clothes, we took a few extra minutes to comb our hair into attractive styles.

While I showered, Sue had called a taxi. And now the driver was tooting his horn outside the hotel entrance.

"Hurry up!" exclaimed my sister. "We can't keep him waiting."

After grabbing our purses, we ran for the elevator. It was early in the morning so we got one right away.

Then we hurried through the lobby and went outside. The taxi driver smiled as we got in. He wasted no time getting through the heavy traffic—finally stopping in front of Madison Avenue Church.

"My, that's a beautiful church," I said to Sue as we climbed out. "I like the beige stone walls and also the neat landscaping."

At that moment the new bright morning pushed back the dark curtain of night. And the sun burst forth in great glory.

As our high heels clicked against the hard concrete walk, Sue paused by one of the flower beds.

"Aren't those red and yellow tulips lovely? After our bleak winter, these spring flowers are so welcome," she added.

We then walked up the brick steps leading to the large glass double doors at the main entrance.

Once inside, we looked around for an empty pew and found one about half way down the long aisle.

I gazed at the front of the sanctuary and whispered to Sue, "Isn't the fragrance of all those lilies simply delightful? They give off a wonderful aroma to the whole building."

"Don't know when I've seen a more artistically decorated church," replied Sue. "The first Easter must have been like this . . . in the garden where His tomb was."

A spirit of awe and reverence permeated the church. As the music from the mighty pipe organ reached our ears, we felt we were on holy ground.

Just before the message, a young tenor soloist sang this song:

> "I saw the Holy City, beside the tideless sea;
> The light of God was on its streets,
> The gates were open wide,
> And all who would might enter,
> And no one was denied.
>
> No need of moon or stars by night;
> Or sun to shine by day,
> It was the New Jerusalem
> That would not pass away."
> (F. E. Weatherly)

According to the bulletin, the pastor's name was Daniel Dahlen. And when he walked to the pulpit, his face beamed with enthusiasm. His text was on the first resurrection when Jesus had triumphed over death and hell. Good Friday's heartbreaking crucifixion scene had now been transformed into the power and glory of Easter Sunday.

Somehow, he caught my attention in a special way and I was really gripped by the message. This man was more than an ordinary minister!

Chapter 23

An Unexpected Call

After the service, Pastor Dahlen went to the foyer to shake hands with the people. When Sue and I met him, he invited us to have breakfast with his congregation in the fellowship hall.

His winning smile made it impossible for us to refuse, and before long several members also came over to welcome us. For a large city congregation, this spirit of warmth and friendliness was remarkable.

We followed the others into the dining area which was filled with individual round tables and chairs. Each table had a vase of freshly cut daffodils on it and we joined the line going to the serving counter. I could hardly wait to taste the golden brown pancakes, little sausages, orange juice and coffee.

After our plates were filled with food, Sue found an empty table.

Then she whispered to me, "Am I ever glad they are providing breakfast here. I'm simply starved and my stomach is growling to prove it."

I smiled at her and put my fork into one of the pancakes.

Later on while we sipped on a second cup of coffee, Pastor Dahlen walked over to our table and sat down.

"Are you ladies going to be living in our fair city?" he asked somewhat cautiously.

Sue beckoned for me to answer him.

"No, I replied, "we are only visitors here for the weekend. My sister is a secretary in Philadelphia and I teach in Fairmont."

"We're delighted to have you both with us on this festive morning. Do come and visit us again real soon," he said. "By the way, may I sit and chat with you for a few minutes?"

"Our pleasure," said Sue.

I couldn't help noticing his appearance. Tall, well-groomed, and his dark hair was styled in the popular crew cut. And from his eyes radiated an inner joy which impressed me no little bit.

After visiting with us for about ten minutes, he left. Then several other families came over to introduce themselves: the Johnsons, Murphys and Radkes.

When we were ready to leave, Sue said, "Isn't it neat to eat in church—on special occasions? And a good way for strangers to get acquainted."

"Say, look around," I added. "We're about the last ones to leave."

As we walked out the main entrance, Sue suggested, "It's such a fine day outside, let's just walk back to the hotel."

"Good idea," I agreed. "We need to enjoy these lovely spring days because the winter months are often too cold for long walks."

While breathing deeply of the balmy April air, Sue said, "Somehow the words sung by the soloist this morning keep running through my mind."

"I don't believe I've ever heard 'The Holy City' sung with more meaning," I replied.

"The sermon was inspiring also," she added. "And, incidentally, one of the members told me that Pastor Dahlen is a widower. His wife died from cancer about three years ago."

"My, that's unfortunate," I answered. "No wonder he spoke with such certainty about the resurrection. He's faced eternity when dealing with his own wife's death."

"No doubt he has struggled through grief . . . like you did after losing Steve," Sue added.

I nodded my head in agreement.

The warm atmosphere must have encouraged the birds to sing more sweetly from the trees as we passed by. And before long we were back at the hotel.

While in the lobby, Sue said to me, "Hey, let's spend the rest of the day talking about old times. So much happened during those years we were apart."

Upon leaving the elevator, we went directly to our room. Sue sat down on a soft chair, looked me squarely in the eye and probed, "By the way . . . did you meet any interesting men while you were overseas?"

"Oh, lots of them," I teased. "But unfortunately, most of them were either married or engaged. However, I must admit I had some delightful dinner dates with none other than our own neighbor, John Arnold."

"You did? Know something . . . I always thought he was so debonair! How come some nice gal hasn't snagged him yet?"

I couldn't help laughing at her candor.

Then I added, "He once told me he had been too occupied with working his way through college to do much dating. And the big war followed and threw all our lives into chaos."

"Hmm . . . do you think he's your type?" she asked.

"I'm not sure, really," I replied. "He was very witty and amusing—but so different from Steve."

"Honey, no one will ever be like Steve. But you can't isolate yourself from other relationships for the rest of your life! You're too young . . . and not bad-looking either," she teased.

"Somehow, I can't get away from this tugging in my heart—to return to Brazil . . . and finish the job we started there years ago."

"Well . . . now . . ."

But before Sue could finish her sentence, we were startled by the sharp ringing of the phone on the night stand.

"Who in the world could that be?" asked Sue. "No one knows we're here except our folks."

"Only one way to find out," I yawned and picked up the receiver.

"Hello," I said.

"Is this you, Ruth?"

"Yes, it is."

"Sorry to bother you, but this is Dan Dahlen of Madison Avenue Church. We met this morning, remember?"

"Yes, yes . . . of course."

"Please, I don't want to appear too forward, but would you like to have dinner with me this evening?"

I was almost too stunned to answer, but finally managed to stammer, "Why, why, I guess that would be possible."

"And bring your sister along, too. I'll be at your hotel at 4:30 this afternoon."

"We'll be ready. And . . . thank you for the invitation."

As I slowly put down the receiver, Sue asked, "Now, Dearie, what was that all about?"

"You won't believe this, but . . . Pastor Dahlen wants both of us to have dinner with him this evening."

"You're kidding!"

"Nope. He was the one on the phone."

"Okay, but *I'm* not going along," she stated, raising her pug nose slightly and defiantly.

"You certainly are! We're both invited."

"Won't hurt you a bit to go without me. Besides . . . in my vast experience, three always ends up being a crowd."

"Won't you change your mind?" I pleaded.

"Not a chance!" she answered stubbornly.

I sighed, but said no more. Sue could be like the Rock of Gibraltar when she wanted to.

So for the next hour, I just stretched out on the soft, wide bed and dozed off.

Surprisingly, I slept soundly and didn't wake up until the distant church clock chimed out four o'clock.

Then I got up, went into the bathroom and splashed cold water on my face. And after brushing my hair, I slipped into the beautiful lavender dress.

After glancing in the mirror, I decided to rearrange my hair into the upsweep style with curls on top. This took more time, of course.

Promptly at 4:30 there was a knock at our door. I answered it. There stood Dan Dahlen with his disarming smile and soon I was walking toward the elevator with my charming escort.

Alone now in our hotel room, Sue chuckled to herself. She had overheard me in the hallway—*trying* to explain why my sister wasn't coming with us.

After stretching and yawning, Sue put on her pink robe and slippers. Then she opened her suitcase where she had tucked away the long novel, *Gone With The Wind.* She curled up in an easy chair by the window and began to read.

Since about 1937, this book had been controversial. Therefore, she wanted to read it for herself before coming to any conclusions. After the previous busy shopping day and then getting up real early this morning, Sue welcomed some quiet hours alone with an interesting book.

An hour later, she called room service. They brought up a delicious dinner which she enjoyed while reading the historical novel, which included the account of the burning of Atlanta.

Even though the book was fascinating, Sue's mind often strayed to other thoughts. How come Pastor Dahlen called up Ruth? Who could predict what he might mean in Ruth's future?

Meanwhile in a quiet, secluded dining room, my dinner with Dan went by very quickly. We talked about many things and before I realized it, seven o'clock had come. Then he drove me back to the hotel because I had a train to catch and he had an evening service.

As soon as I returned, we hurriedly packed our suitcases.

Finally, Sue looked intently at me and asked, "My, you're quiet. What happened at dinner?"

I smiled at her but didn't answer.

"I've already called a cab," she added, "and he should be here any minute. Can't miss our trains, you know."

After climbing into the taxi, we had another fast ride through the crowded city traffic. But we got to the station safely—and on time.

As Sue was about to board her train to Philly, she kissed me goodbye and walked up into the passenger car. The first one was already filled so she went on to the second. There, the only available seat was one next to an elderly, obese lady. Sue managed to squeeze in between this woman and the window. *This could be one long, uncomfortable ride back,* she thought to herself.

Meanwhile at the depot, I had to wait another ten minutes before my train to Fairmont chugged into the terminal. I climbed aboard with my luggage. But this passenger car had plenty of room so I put my suitcase on the shelf above me and had a double seat to myself.

I really hoped that this ride home would be a quiet one. So many conflicting thoughts raced through my head that needed sorting out.

But before I realized what had happened, weariness overtook me and I fell sound asleep. The hour fled by and soon I heard the train screech to a sudden halt as the conductor called out, "Fairmont!"

Because we lived only a short distance away, I walked home instead of calling Dad for a ride.

But as soon as I got into the kitchen, he said, "My dear, why didn't you let me know when your train got in? I would have gladly picked you up."

"No problem," I answered. "Besides . . . it was good to walk in the fresh, clean air—after a weekend in the Big City."

Mother then came into the kitchen and asked, "How was Sue? And the trip?"

"Simply great! I never realized how quickly she has grown up. We needed this time together—having been apart for so many years."

"By the way," queried Dad as we sat around the table drinking some coffee, "were you able to attend church today?"

"Actually . . . we did. And found the people at Madison Avenue Church to be warm and friendly. Even had breakfast there."

"But you must be tired by now," added Mother. "Perhaps you should get some rest now and we'll talk more in the morning."

"I'm all for that," I yawned, "and tomorrow will soon be here. We have school also—no Easter Monday off this year 'cause of too many vacation days during the January blizzards."

I pulled myself upstairs using the handrail, sat down on my bed and kicked off my shoes. With my lesson plans all done, I took a quick shower and crawled into bed.

Suddenly, I thought of the new curtains. *Oh, well, I'll give them to Mom the first thing tomorrow morning,* I thought.

But for some reason, I couldn't get to sleep. I heard the clock strike twelve, one, and two—then I dozed off.

The bright sunshine of the new day awakened me before my alarm went off. I could hardly wait to get dressed and give the pretty curtains to Mom.

She was already preparing breakfast in the kitchen when I handed her the package.

"Sue helped me pick these out for you," I said.

"You shouldn't have done this," she answered while hurriedly unwrapping the gift.

At once she held one up to a window.

"They're simply lovely!" she exclaimed. "Why . . . they'll just transform this whole kitchen. Thank you both—ever so much."

"Will they fit?" I asked.

After doing some measuring, she continued, "Honestly, I don't believe we need to do any altering on these."

We spent the next half hour taking down the old curtains and putting up the new ones.

"Nothing could have pleased me more," replied Mother as she gave me a warm hug. "During the war years, we didn't feel much like sprucing up the house. Instead, we saved all we could and bought War Bonds."

"They even look good to me!" exclaimed Dad with a twinkle in his eyes. Mother had always done the inside decorating of the house, while Dad kept up the lawn and flowers outside.

After breakfast, I hurried to school. But I had a difficult time concentrating in my classes. Conflicting thoughts were jumping around inside my head. What did it all mean?

Chapter 24

THE Letter

In a few short weeks came May with final exams and graduation of the Lincoln High Class of 1947. Those days in May had been so full of activities that I often wondered if I'd survive until the term ended. And this spring, with the war over, more than half of the seniors had already registered for college or tech school in the fall.

However, the very day after graduation, a mysterious letter came in the mail for me. The return address was . . . "Madison Avenue Church of New York City."

Bubbling over with curiosity, I slit open the envelope, took out the letter and blinked my eyes in astonishment. It read:

"Dear Ruth,

"It was a real joy to meet you and your sister on Easter Sunday. And our dinner together that evening was so special!

"I was also impressed by the work you did in linguistics with that primitive tribe in Brazil—as well as your job overseas with the Army Intelligence Department.

"Now, please don't misunderstand what I am about to say. Before writing this letter, I gave much time to prayer and seeking God's Will.

"I have not been able to get you out of my heart and thoughts since our dinner together. In fact, for the first time in my life, it has been difficult to concentrate on my regular parish duties. May I tell you sincerely that 'I love you' and would be honored to have you become my wife.

"Please pray about this proposal. We both want the Lord's will to be done. But don't take too long before answering it.

With all my love,

Dan"

In utter shock, I sat down on my bed and reread the letter. Then I raced down the stairway.

"Mother, I simply can't believe this! Imagine the nerve of this man proposing to me by mail! Have you seen anything so unromantic? I know now what my answer will be. No . . . no . . . no . . . !"

"My dear," asked my bewildered Mother, "whatever are you talking about?"

"This letter . . . why, why it's a written proposal of marriage from Pastor Dan Dahlen of New York City."

She paused for a few minutes to think, then said, "Well, my dear, let's not be so hasty. I have lived much longer than you and have sometimes seen the Lord work out His plans in mighty strange and mysterious ways."

I couldn't answer that, so in disgust I stomped back upstairs to my room and tossed that letter into the bottom drawer of my desk.

In the following days we never mentioned the mysterious letter. Then a week later as my parents were having a second cup of coffee after breakfast and I had gone downtown to shop, Dad said, "Ruth surely doesn't act like herself these days."

"Perhaps that letter from Pastor Dahlen has upset her more than we realize. But I do hope she will at least pray about it before answering . . . or ignoring it altogether!" added Mother.

Earlier in March, I had signed up for some summer courses at the American University in Washington, D.C. I needed these for renewal of my teaching certificate.

So on June 3, I packed a couple of suitcases and took the afternoon train to our nation's Capital.

I had always had a desire to visit this historic place. And a few weeks ago, John Arnold had written and encouraged me to come to Washington when our school term was over.

D.C. had a reputation of being hot and humid in the summer, but I *hoped* this June might be tolerable at least.

From the train depot I took a cab to the campus and soon was assigned a corner room on second floor of the girls' dorm.

The first few days were hectic as I learned where my classes were held, but I did manage to get acquainted with some of the students there.

When the first tough week of classes was finally over, I realized that Friday evening was unusually quiet. Why not call John? After all, I still had five more weeks of summer school left.

After dialing his number, I was pleased to find him home.

He said, "Why, Ruth, is it really you? I'm so glad to hear your voice again."

"Am I calling at a bad time?" I asked.

"Not at all. I'm only reading a magazine and that can wait."

"I've just finished my first week of school," I added, "and wondered how things were going for you."

"Great!" he exclaimed. "Just love my new job and this city is beyond words! By the way, I've got a couple of tickets for the big baseball game tomorrow night. Care to go with me?"

"Sure do," I answered. "You know I love baseball—and would love to get away from the books for an evening also."

"Pick you up at seven. Are you in the dorm?"

"Yes . . . and am I ever glad you have those tickets!"

Saturday I busied myself doing some laundry and cleaning up my room. The thought of going out to a game in the evening made me feel like singing and even the chores seemed rather enjoyable.

About ten to seven that evening, I went outside and sat on a bench under a cool shade tree. The heat in the dorm had become most uncomfortable.

In a few minutes John drove up in a sleek new maroon Chrysler. As he jumped out of the car he walked up to me and said, "Can't believe it's really you, Ruth!"

He could be charming when he wanted to and his brown eyes really twinkled tonight.

I looked at him and smiled as he escorted me to his car. While driving to the ballpark, I thought to myself, *What charisma this fellow has!*

The weather was perfect with a gentle breeze blowing across the field from first to third base. The vendors were selling all kinds of things. So John bought us some hot dogs and cokes.

While sipping on my iced coke, I asked him, "Didn't you miss the college games during the war?"

"You bet! But I missed a lot of things more back in the good old U.S.A.—like having Christmas with my family. By the way, how do you like your courses at the U.?"

"Most of them are interesting," I answered, "but honestly, it's tough to study late in the evenings again."

"Competition pretty keen?" he asked.

"A lot stiffer now than when I was in college. These former GIs are more mature and serious about getting an education."

"You can say that again. Before the war, lots of kids just went to school for a good time, especially the rich ones," he added.

I agreed.

"Funny thing," he continued, "I thought I was quite grown-up after finishing college, but those years in the Army showed me how little I knew about life in general."

"Changing the subject," I said, "the game is now tied at 5-all, and this is the end of the ninth. How many more innings do you think it'll take before we win—or they?"

"Don't know, but let's stay until one team does."

John then bought us some hot buttered popcorn. It was yummy! And the cool breeze now blowing was more than welcome.

"Sure have met some terrific people here in D.C.," he went on. "Incidentally, would you like a tour of the Capitol and Lincoln's Memorial one of these days?"

"Sure would. Can we see the White House, too?"

"*That* is one beautiful place! Only trouble—the tour guides take people through much too fast," he replied.

It took three more innings before Washington won the game, 6 to 5, so it was about midnight before John drove me back to the dorm.

"I'll call you real soon," he added tenderly as he held my hand at the door.

"Thanks for a marvelous evening," I added, feeling almost giddy inside. After walking up the stairway to my room, I crawled into bed, but couldn't sleep. I just tossed restlessly until the clock struck 3 a.m. Then I got up, grabbed an economics book and hoped it would bore me to sleep.

After opening the large textbook, the faces of John and Dan seemed to appear on every page I read. What a fun time I'd had with John this evening. He was both charming and witty—and his family had been our neighbors for years. Yet, why was there this invisible barrier between us?

Deep down, I believe I knew the answer. When only a teenager, I had trusted Jesus Christ as my personal Savior and wanted Him to direct my life. Unfortunately, whenever I tried to witness about Christ in my life, John skillfully changed the subject.

Then suddenly I remembered the inspiring Easter service at Madison Avenue Church. What a warm and caring spirit there had been! And Dan had also expressed great interest in the work Steve and I had begun with the Amazon tribe. In addition, I had experienced a real romantic chemistry between Dan and me during our special dinner together.

But why hadn't some other couple gone to Brazil to carry on our work? Of course, World War II had made a big difference. Mission Boards were not sending out missionaries when so many ships were being sunk. But . . . those dear natives must still be waiting to hear the Gospel in their own language.

What should I do now? Actually, what does the Lord want me to do?

Then this verse of Scripture flashed across my mind: "Be ye not unequally yoked together with unbelievers" (II Cor. 6:14).

A high school friend of mine, Margie, found herself in an unhappy marriage because she had thought physical attraction was sufficient grounds for a good marriage. She was wrong and a traumatic divorce had been devastating to her two dear little children.

I must have slept only one hour—before the alarm went off on Sunday morning. Though feeling a bit groggy, I got up, dressed and ate breakfast. While hurrying off to church, I thought perhaps I might get some answers there.

Also I needed to reply to Dan's letter . . . one way or another . . . and soon.

Monday morning I went to my classes as usual. But because of little sleep during the weekend, I wasn't too sharp in my studies.

Later on that afternoon in my dorm room, I was studying for a test when the hallway phone rang.

Annette, who lived a few doors down from me, answered it. Then she shouted out, "Hey, Ruth, it's for you."

Who could that be? I wondered as I hurried to pick up the receiver. It was John Arnold.

He asked, "Say, how about going with me to the symphony tonight? I know this is short notice, but I just bought two tickets this noon. Beethoven's music will be featured, too."

"Oh, John, I'd really love to go because he's one of my favorite composers," I replied, "but I'm sorry I can't."

"Why not?"

"There's an important letter on my desk that I must answer . . . tonight."

"Tonight? Can't it wait?" John could scarcely believe his ears, but managed to add, "Well . . . okay, then . . . some other time, perhaps."

As he gently put down the receiver, John took a deep breath and shook his head. A letter more important than a symphony concert? Who would ever understand women, anyhow? And Ruth and I seemed to have such a good time at the ball game.

At any rate, I'll probably call her again next week, he mused. Maybe she wasn't feeling well and would be in a better mood later on. Strange, though . . . it is not like her to be moody. However, I simply must find out more about this mysterious letter that was more important than a date with me!

Meanwhile back in my room, I pulled out Dan's letter of proposal. It had been collecting dust for several weeks.

After more earnest prayer, I came to the conclusion that this letter had been arranged by the Lord, and it was His way of bringing happiness to both of us.

If I married Dan, we could then return together to finish the task in Brazil. Those precious natives needed to hear the answer to life's most important question . . . In whom do I find eternal life?